"I only wish I had this insightful book to read when my son was diagnosed with Type 1 diabetes. Those first few weeks and months are among the scariest we will ever face. Karen put into words much of what I experienced. This book serves 2 purposes: First, to validate our concerns and fears and to let us know we are not alone. Secondly, to help break through the mystery of how to take the leading role in dealing with school, coaches, neighbors, playmates and all those who touch our child's lives. Even when you think you have it all figured out, this book will serve as a terrific resource to refer to on an ongoing basis."

—Liz Cartini, Parent of a child with Type1 Diabetes

"WOW, this book is a fantastic resource for parents and loved ones of newly diagnosed Type 1 diabetics. The book is not only full of useful and easy to understand information but it speaks to you from the heart and in a time when your life has been turned upside down it is good to know that you are not alone and the rollercoaster you are about to ride is normal. When my son was diagnosed 2 ½ years ago, at the age of 4, I searched for this type of information and could not find it; it would have made life a lot easier if I had resource as good as this one. This book is a must have in your library of diabetic information."

—Cheryl Fassett, Mother of a child with Type1 Diabetes

"No one can understand the impact of diabetes until they have lived through it. This book tells a story in a way that makes you part of the family. Hopefully other families especially those that are newly diagnosed will benefit from its strength and love."

—Lucienne Cole-Dargan, Executive Director, Central New York Chapter, Juvenile Diabetes Research Foundation.

My Child Has Diabetes

My Child Has Diabetes

✦

A Parent's Guide to a Normal Life After Diagnosis

Karen Hargrave-Nykaza

iUniverse, Inc.
New York Lincoln Shanghai

My Child Has Diabetes
A Parent's Guide to a Normal Life After Diagnosis

iUniverse books may be ordered through booksellers or by contacting:

iUniverse
2021 Pine Lake Road, Suite 100
Lincoln, NE 68512
www.iuniverse.com
1-800-Authors (1-800-288-4677)

ISBN-13: 978-0-595-38841-7 (pbk)
ISBN-13: 978-0-595-83219-4 (ebk)
ISBN-10: 0-595-38841-8 (pbk)
ISBN-10: 0-595-83219-9 (ebk)

Printed in the United States of America

For Joel…You have amazed us with your bravery since the day you were diagnosed. We love you so much.

For Kevin, Casey, and all children and families living with diabetes.

Contents

This book is written by a woman with no medical training whatsoever. Although the author lists many things that she does to manage her own son's diabetes, these techniques are used specifically for her son, and are listed here only as examples. This book is not to be interpreted as medical advice in any way. Nothing the reader finds here should be used unless the reader checks with his or her child's own doctor.

I would like to thank my family for their support while I wrote this book. Joel, Casey and Kevin, I love you. We have all come a long way since that first day. Joel set the standard high with his acceptance of diabetes into his life and his amazing skills and knowledge. I hope we can each do as well as he does every day.

Thank you, Mom, for going outside your comfort zone to learn more about diabetes, and to know so much that you can take care of Joel for days at a time. You and Donna mean so much to all of us.

Thank you, Maggie for coming into my life at the exact time I needed you. Thank you for caring, for learning everything about diabetes and for being willing to care for Joel. Thank you for supporting me and our family in every way that you possibly can. Each member of your family offers us such giving and open friendship. Thank you, Eve, Gwen, Rose and Bill, for your friendship and acceptance. We never feel "different" because of diabetes in the company of true friends.

Thank you, Dad, for reminding me that life is too short not to go after your dreams. You and Mom made me believe that I could do anything I wanted to do. I just did!

Foreword

I used to think that there was nothing tougher than living with diabetes. After all, I've tried (with limited success) to manage my own for the past 21 years. But having worked with many parents of children with diabetes, I now realize that my own challenges pale in comparison to yours.

In caring for a child with diabetes, you get to deal with all the usual hassles associated with daily diabetes care—unexpected highs & lows, frequent blood sugar checks, having to count carbs in every morsel of food, adjustments for physical activity, and so on. But as an added bonus, you also have to contend with growth, pubertal hormones, school personnel/camp counselors/babysitters, hypersensitivity (or resistance) to food & insulin, mood changes, and complex family dynamics. Plus, as parents, we have that constant sense of *responsibility* and *accountability* for everything that can, and does, go wrong. If my own blood sugar is high or low, I deal with it and move on. But when a child's blood sugar is high or low, parents tend to take it very personally.

By now you have surely discovered that diabetes is not something that your doctor or nurse is going to take care of for you. You, as parents and caregivers, are the ones managing this disease for your child. Not that your health care team doesn't play an important role, but you are the ones in the trenches day in and day out making the important decisions and carrying out the critical tasks.

My Child has Diabetes is written by a **parent**—a true expert in what it takes to deal with a child's diabetes. Who else is else going to tell you that you don't have to make friends with the school principal? Which battles are worth fighting, and which are best left alone? That letting your child be a kid is really more important than diabetes management?

Karen Hargrave puts everyday situations into the proper perspective and provides practical solutions. She also doesn't let you forget to maintain your own personal balance while taking care of your child. Hearing Karen's personal story and reliving her successes (and failures) will help to inspire, motivate and equip you to better handle the challenges that lie ahead.

I'm lucky. None of my four kids has diabetes. But I still get nervous every time one of them starts going to the bathroom a lot (come here, let me check something…). But if my worst fears ever do come true, at least I know that there are resources…heck, an entire community…here to help me handle the toughest job of all.

To Karen and all the parents out there who commit their every ounce of energy to doing the best job possible for their children, here's to you!

Gary Scheiner, MS, CDE

Introduction

This book came about as a result of my own frustration while looking for exactly this type of book. Although I found plenty of books about the medical aspects of diabetes, what I needed was a how-to guide for all the things that come up daily that doctors and nurses either don't have the time for, or don't think to tell you. I didn't need another book with photos of syringes and detailed information on counting carbs and administering shots and glucagon. I found myself asking my husband, "Where is the expert who can tell me exactly what information I need to provide for school and how to handle a birthday party without making Joel stand out from all of his peers because his mother has to stay at the party?" I searched for an up-to-date reference for how to handle the issues and paperwork needed for everything to be in place at school, getting emotional support for your family, maintaining control over diabetes without obsessing over it and keeping your child's life "normal" despite diabetes. I found bits and pieces of this information in books that I read, but it was never everything I needed, and never all in one book.

As time went on after my son was first diagnosed, it turned out that the school wasn't going to come to me and tell me exactly what I needed to do as I had naively expected. I had no idea whether it was safe for my son to ride his bike to his friend's house alone. And did we really have to carry this glucagon with us every time we left the house? I didn't find the answers to these and so many other questions anywhere. I learned as I went along, and then wrote my own book.

The support for you as a parent of a child with diabetes is there, but you really have to look for it. This book will answer many of your questions as well as provide the emotional support you need.

PART I

Adjusting to Life with Diabetes

1

Life-Changing Moments: The Diagnosis

None of us will ever forget the time, date, place and way our child was diagnosed with diabetes. It was the moment that their lives and ours changed forever. I remember thinking that it must not really be happening because the world was still going on as if everything were normal. Surely since MY child had just developed a life threatening disease, people would stop what they were doing, much as they did on 9/11. Without minimizing the horror of the families of those who lost their lives that day, that is the kind of paralyzing tragedy it was for me, even though we were talking about one child who was still alive, not thousands of people who had lost their lives. When it is your child, it feels like the world should stop turning.

I often think of that day as the day my son lost his childhood and his ability to be carefree. He lost it forever. Never again would he be able to just run down the street to a friend's house without giving a thought to having a testing kit, supplies and snacks with him. He would always need to be aware of how he was feeling, where his supplies were, that he had snacks and juice available and that everything he does or feels would affect his blood sugar. That is a lot of responsibility for a 7 year-old, and about as far away from carefree as you can get. It was so unfair. He is the most loving, easy-going child and this was such a raw deal.

Before my son Joel was diagnosed, he was wetting the bed for the first time in his life. He was so excited about the start of the new school year, we guessed it was from that. He was drinking and eating constantly, but what 7 year-old boy doesn't? He was having headaches, but we had been told that he would need glasses at his next doctor's appointment. I almost called the doctor the first time he wet the bed, but decided they would just tell me to have him cut back on drinking after dinner. We tried to do that. I didn't know it at the time, but his body needed all of that water because he now had diabetes and his body was full of excess glucose.

One morning he had another headache and just didn't look right to me. I called the pediatrician and told the nurse what was happening. She told me to bring him right in. At this point, I was thinking that the glasses couldn't wait and that would probably be our next stop. The doctor opened his chart and said, "He has lost 5 pounds. That is big for someone his size." Then the panic started. He was looking for something major to be wrong. He checked a couple of other things and then had Joel give a urine sample. We waited for what seemed like hours, but it was only a couple of minutes. The doctor came back into the room and said, "That will teach you to bring him to the doctor for headaches: he's got diabetes." I will never forget those words or that moment. Our lives would never be the same.

The pediatrician told me that I should expect a 2-3 day hospital stay. We would need to go immediately once they arranged it by phone. I had never gotten such fast service from the staff at the Doctor's office. I knew it had to be an emergency the way they were moving. The doctor came back in and said we would be going to the Joslin Center instead. I had been trying to reach my husband, Kevin, and couldn't. He was working nights that week and was home sleeping. The doctor said I did not have time to go tell him, I had to go right from there. I called my Mom and told her she needed to be strong for what I was about to tell her. I think I was trying to tell myself to be strong. I told her about the diagnosis and that I needed her to go get Kevin and have him meet us there. Then she would have to pick up our other son at preschool for us. I was holding myself together quite well: I had to. Joel was watching me very closely, and I knew he was taking his cues of how to react from me.

As the doctor told me what would be involved in having diabetes, I tried to tell Joel. He explained that he would need to test his blood 5-6 times a day and take shots 3-4 times a day. Joel heard all this and asked, "For how long?" Then I realized that anything he had ever been treated for medically had been temporary. This was different. I looked him in the eye and said, "Forever…or until they find a cure." I told him that I was afraid too, but as the doctor had just told us, this was treatable and we were going to go learn what to do together. He just looked at me and said, "OK." Until you have witnessed it yourself firsthand, you have no idea how resilient and adaptable kids are. It is a cliché, but it is amazing how true it is. Neither Joel nor I shed a single tear that first day. I am not bragging here, just stating a fact that I still can't believe or understand.

He and I went downtown to the Joslin Center together and they took us in right away. My mind was still spinning. I wasn't even sure how I had made the 20 minute drive from the pediatrician's office. In times of crisis I guess you just go on autopilot, but I still couldn't believe what was happening. I was now in the position of needing to learn things on which my son's life would depend. I was trying to force myself to focus, but I felt like I was watching someone's worst nightmare. The doctor came in and began to explain what diabetes was, how it developed and what we would need to do to treat it to stabilize Joel. When we first arrived at Joslin they took Joel's blood sugar and took a urine sample. The blood glucose meter read "high" which I was told meant that it was over 600. I really had no understanding of how high that was until days later. They also told me that Joel had ketones in his urine. I had no idea what that meant either. It is just as well I didn't know at the time just how dangerous that was. I was not a medical person at all, and didn't want to become one. I was beginning to realize that I had no choice. I was also beginning to resent that very much.

The nurse, Kathy, came in next and boiled everything down for me as much as she could. I just couldn't believe all that I was hearing, all that we would need to do just to keep Joel alive. Our world had completely changed in such a short time. Kevin arrived at the Joslin Center just as Joel and I were going out to the snack bar. He looked like a train had hit him, he had obviously been crying, yet I was still totally composed. This was truly a sign that our world must be collapsing. Not only was our son very sick, but we had completely reversed roles. He should have been the strong one, while I had the nervous break down. That reaction would have felt somewhat normal.

Kevin, Joel and I went back into the office to learn all that we could from Kathy. At one point I took her aside and said something like, "I know this is not about me, but I don't do needles and I don't think I can do this." She said that I would have to, or we would have to take Joel to the hospital instead of taking him home. I would just have to do it, so I did. She had Kevin and I give each other shots to practice, and we did it! Then we had to give Joel his first shot. She told me to do it. I thought I would pass out, but I did my best to hide my fear from Joel and did it. A while later it was Kevin's turn, and he gave Joel a shot. He was trying to be brave too, but at this point we were all faking it.

Kathy continued to flood us with information that we would be using immediately to regulate Joel's blood sugar and to keep him alive. Suddenly it was going to be a daily effort to keep him alive. That is such a foreign concept for someone who has had a perfectly healthy child for 7 ½ years. That health is no longer automatic and that takes getting used to. Over the course of that endless afternoon, my mind continued to wander back to that same thought. If I couldn't learn how to take care of Joel, he could die. As we prepared to take Joel home that afternoon, it really seemed that he should be spending the night in the hospital where people knew how to care for him. But Kathy said we should take him home to make life as normal as possible. We were as far away from normal as we had ever been.

All day I had been telling Joel that maybe Dad would get him a new game for his Game boy. It seemed like such a small thing to us but it had served as an effective distraction for Joel throughout a very long day. So as we left, Kevin took Joel to the mall while I headed for the drugstore to get the rest of the supplies we would need. I couldn't even identify all of these things yet; how was I supposed to know what to do with them? There was so much stuff. Where would we put it all? How were we going to remember how to use it? As soon as we got home, it was time to eat. Oh no, here we go! Already we needed to figure out how much insulin to give him. His blood sugar was 595 when we left Joslin, still dangerously high. The doctor said that the ketones were gone from his urine and that was important. Somebody remind me what a ketone is please. I know it is important and very hard to understand if you are not a scientist, but I couldn't remember. So now we were in charge of regulating his blood sugar. Something we would be doing for every minute of every day for the rest of his life.

We got through the first night with testing him multiple times during the night, something we would be doing for at least the first few weeks. That first day my husband made a mistake with the insulin dose he gave Joel. He was devastated. I quickly forgave him, knowing that I would make a mistake too at some point; we all would. In a way, it was good for us to see that even when we made a mistake Joel was OK. We were overwhelmed, sleep deprived and always up and down emotionally. Our mood was directly linked to Joel's blood sugar. When it was good, we were so relieved. When it was bad, we panicked.

Something I remember vividly from those first few days was the overwhelming feeling that I had to get away from the diabetes and just couldn't. No matter what I tried to do to relax it was always there. It was an amazing feeling once

Kevin and I finally got comfortable with just one of us taking care of Joel on our own for a couple of hours. Once that happened the other person could escape the house for a much needed break. For the first few days it was a two-parent job, no exceptions. We consulted on everything.

And yes, Joel does have a sibling who was a challenging 4 year-old at the time, and that was on a good day. Imagine how challenging he became when his brother was getting all this attention. He found a number of ways to let us know that he wasn't getting his share of attention, the most creative of which was to develop "pretend diabetes" himself. We got both him and Joel each a play medical kit and Casey began "testing" and "taking shots" just like Joel. It actually was a pretty therapeutic thing for everyone at the time.

The next day we talked to a lot of family members. I couldn't believe how much it helped when someone called or sent a card or e-mail, but it really did. We were also back at the drugstore and grocery store. I think I spent over $600 on groceries in the first 2 weeks. Food felt like our best friend and worst enemy at the same time. Now we just had to figure out what he needed, when he needed it and how much he needed! It all seemed so contradictory. I was supposed to watch his carbohydrate and sugar intake, but everything they told me to buy for him for snacks was full of carbs. One of us was going to weigh 200 pounds by the end of the month and I was pretty sure it was me.

I also went into Joel's school to meet with the school nurse, his teacher and the school counselor. They took me into the counselor's office and the nurse asked me how Joel was doing. I started to tell them in great detail how strong he had been. The counselor then asked me, "But how are YOU doing?" Apparently, that was my cue, because I burst into tears for the first time since he had been diagnosed the day before. It felt good to get it out, especially in the presence of someone who didn't need me to give anything back. She was just there for me, which was great. She offered to be there for me anytime I needed to talk. It seemed like we would all have a lot of support at school, which I knew was going to be very important.

Keeping Joel's blood sugar regulated was our main objective each day of that whole first week or so. He was diagnosed on a Thursday and was back in school the following Monday. He had an amazing teacher that year. If it were not for her, I don't know that I could have put him back in school so quickly. The first thing she said to me that day was that her father had type 1 diabetes too. Thank

God, one person to whom I didn't have to teach an entire new language to. She "got it," and as I was about to learn, not many people did. I never worried about him once I knew he was at school under her care. That is saying a lot considering how worried I was at that point. Joel thrived in her class not only because she is an exceptional teacher, but because she is an exceptional person.

I think when your child is diagnosed with diabetes (and I imagine any chronic illness), you go through a mourning process for your healthy child. Your healthy child is gone, there is no question about it. I have heard this expressed by other parents of diabetic children and I think it is something those parents of healthy children have a hard time understanding. They think that because diabetes is treatable we are somehow "lucky" that our child can live a relatively normal life. We should be grateful that it isn't cancer or another disease that possibly cannot be treated or cured. I realize that we are lucky in that way. We have had friends whose children have been diagnosed with cancer. It reminds us to be grateful that Joel "has only diabetes." A child with cancer obviously faces a significant chance of not surviving despite all of the treatment they receive. But the truth is that they also face the chance of putting their cancer behind them at some point, although I am sure it never really feels that way to them and their families. I am sure they are constantly worried about the cancer returning. I would never want to lessen or minimize all that a child with cancer and their family goes through, especially the very serious threat to their life. But Joel's diabetes isn't ever going away and there is no break from it. It isn't a contest of who suffers most, it is just different. I don't know of another disease that requires the kind of constant monitoring that diabetes demands. Only another parent who lives with this disease every day can truly understand the pervasive impact it has on your life every minute of every day. Your child being robbed of their healthy childhood and life fills you with an anger and anxiety that can't be put into words. It also can't be easily understood by those who aren't living it. I wish it were something that I didn't have a reason to understand.

2

The Learning and Adjustment

The day Joel was diagnosed, the pediatrician said to me, "In a month you are going to know more about diabetes than I do." I found that so hard to believe. When we got to the Joslin Center, Kathy, Joel's nurse, said, "In a few months you are going to be calling me to tell me what adjustments need to be made to his doses of insulin." Didn't they realize that I had NO medical background or experience? How was I possibly going to understand all of this, much less be able to tell a doctor or nurse something? Suddenly I was not qualified to care for my own child. This was a whole other emotion to be dealing with. I was a capable person and a good mother. This terrible disease was making me feel incapable. And a month didn't sound like very long to retain all of this information and be able to calculate and comprehend doses that Joel would need.

We learned a lot that first week and we did manage to retain most of it. I didn't let myself look too much in books or on websites because when I did, I was just reminded of all that I didn't know. Kathy said we needed to concentrate on only the basics at this point, so that was what we did. I also had asked her about all of the horrible complications you hear about that can happen for people with diabetes. She said that for people who manage their diabetes those complications won't happen. I couldn't tell if she was just telling me that because she knew I couldn't handle any more bad news, or if that was really true. I was going to go with it for now, because I couldn't handle any more bad news.

I found it very difficult that we were determining how much insulin Joel needed by trial and error. It felt like we were using him as a guinea pig, because we were. Kathy explained that there was no other way to figure out how much of each kind of insulin he would need to keep his blood sugar level. She assured us that all the fluctuating we would see in his blood sugars would be safe. It didn't seem like it could be, but we didn't have a choice. We also needed to figure out how much he would need to "cover his food". He would get one dose of long acting insulin to carry him through the day and night, and then he would receive short acting insulin in a ratio to the amount of food he was eating. There was so much to figure out and they made it very clear to us from the beginning that it was all subject to change at any time. Everything was going to affect his blood sugar: stress, growth, exercise, carbs, fat, etc.

No one adjusted to Joel's diabetes better or faster than Joel. He amazed us by testing his blood on his own that first day and even giving himself a shot the second day. There was no complaining and there were almost no tears. It was completely amazing considering how terrible he must have felt physically. His blood sugar was still going up and down like crazy. Kevin and I took turns losing it over this new life we were trying to get used to while Joel went calmly on, adjusting like a pro. It was a huge relief to us that it seemed to be easier on him than it was on us.

The thing about diabetes is that it has its own language. All of a sudden you need to become fluent in all of these medical terms: novolog, NPH, ketones, bolus, basal, site change, glucagon, A1C, honeymoon phase, etc. I was having a hard time remembering which type of insulin was which and all the terminology was really throwing me off. But like everything else, we got it eventually.

The "language barrier" as I will refer to it here, is also one of the most alienating things when trying to talk to someone about diabetes. If you don't live with the disease in your home or work in the field of diabetes care, you would have no reason to be familiar with any of the terms that are used to describe the daily management of diabetes. This makes it almost impossible to answer the question, "How is Joel?" without sounding like you are trying to teach someone a whole new language. When you come back with something like, "His basal rate was off so we gave him a bolus at 2am," it is no wonder that your friends look at you a little funny. They don't know what you are talking about!

The problem with this language barrier is that there are no other words you can use to substitute for the words that are used to describe diabetes care. So you either have to get used to those funny looks, enjoy feeling smart because you now sound like a doctor or find at least one friend who is willing to learn enough about it in order for you to have someone to talk to about it.

Another thing that really got us in the beginning was how you could never leave the house without all the diabetes "stuff". It was just amazing that we always had to have a meter, glucagon, snacks, juice, frosting, insulin, syringes and more. A walk across the street became an event. A trip out for dinner became a HUGE event that honestly didn't seem worth the trouble. Just when we had graduated to life without a diaper bag, now we had a diabetes bag. But that got easier with time too.

We found out from the school nurse that there was another child at our son's school who had diabetes. Her mother was a nurse and she was very helpful getting the kids introduced to each other and sharing some information with us as parents. It made an enormous difference to all of us just to know that there was someone else with diabetes right at his school. Immediately he felt less different and less alone. Abby (the child with diabetes at his school) even came down to the nurse's office on Joel's first day back to school while he tested his blood for the first time at school. Somehow having another kid going through it made it easier, and for that we will always be so thankful. Eventually Joel and Abby had a routine of testing, comparing blood sugars and passing each other in the nurse's office.

Something that Abby's Mom suggested is that I go into the classroom with Joel as she had done with Abby, to explain diabetes to the kids in his class. Within a week or so, I arranged with Joel's teacher to do just that. We explained to the kids what diabetes was by reading his class the book, *Taking Diabetes to School.* After hearing the story they could ask questions, and boy, did they ask questions! Then Joel showed them how he tested his blood, which had them completely fascinated. The class learned that they cannot "catch" diabetes from Joel, that he is a normal kid and that he wants to be their friend like everyone else. I have gone into his class the first month of school to talk to the class every year since his diagnosis, and it really makes a difference when the other kids understand what he is doing and why.

Other parents don't really know what to say when you tell them that your child has diabetes. It was surprising to me that kids seem to handle it much easier. Sometimes adults just don't know what to say. You hear some pretty stupid comments and most come from people not being educated about the disease. Try to remember that many of us were not educated about diabetes until we had to be either. If you are unhappy with how little your friends and family know about diabetes, help educate them. Invite them to a Diabetes Family Education Weekend, offer to share your books or online sources with them and just spend time with them. Being around your child is the best way for them to see what it is really all about. By being around you they will see firsthand how much there is to do just to live daily life with diabetes. There are so many misconceptions about diabetes, my least favorite being that you get it "under control" and there is little fluctuation in the blood sugar once it is under control. Again, the key to doing away with such misconceptions is education.

In my opinion, one of the most important parts of learning to adjust to parenting a child with diabetes is taking care of you. This seems to be something of an oxymoron. Your child has a disease that most likely no one but you knows how to care for and now you want to get out on your own. Who are you supposed to leave him/her with? You need to be creative about your options. You will be of no use to your child if you are burned out and exhausted. Chapter 6 deals with this subject exclusively.

PART II

What You Need to Do for School

3

The School Nurse, Principal, Your Child's Teacher and the Dreaded School Field Trip

"I don't need the principal to be my friend. I have a lot of friends. What I need is for him to make a mental connection between me and Joel having diabetes. That way every time he sees me or hears from me, he is reminded that he must do what he needs to do to keep Joel safe in school."

This is something that I said to a friend of mine after a conflict I had with a principal over an issue where Joel's safety was concerned. If you find yourself in a situation such as this one, you may need to make a very uncomfortable phone call to the principal or administrator to clarify what needs to be done in the future to keep your child safe. If after such efforts, your expectations are still not met, you may find that you need to follow up that phone call with a letter outlining your disappointment and what issues need to be addressed immediately, again to ensure your child's safety. If you have no luck with the principal or administrator, you can let the administrator know that your next letter will be going to the school board. It is amazing what lightning fast service you will suddenly get. After such actions have been taken on your part, I think it is safe to say that the important connection I referred to at the beginning of this chapter has been made: the connection between you and your principal knowing he needs to keep your child safe. It is also safe to say that you may not be friends. This is okay. This is not his role in your life and you may need to remind yourself of that.

I give this example because I think most parents who have a diabetic child will find that, from time to time, they need to be a vocal advocate for their child's rights at school or elsewhere. I also give this example because it is hard to remind yourself what role these important people at school play in your life and your child's life. It is not that of a friend. If you are a "people pleaser" by nature this will be even more of a challenge. Not everyone is going to like what you have to say, especially if you need to demand proper care or treatment for your child because the school is not adequately meeting your child's needs without your intervention. Accepting that not everyone is going to like you or think you are easy to deal with is a difficult process, but it is a necessary one for so many areas of life. This is one of those areas.

Before Joel's diagnosis, the school nurse was never someone I expected to get to know very well. I didn't expect that my children would need much more from her than the occasional band-aid or call to home when they were sick. I expected to know the school principal even less. Since my children haven't been trouble-makers, I didn't anticipate a reason that I would get to know him very well either. I had always hoped to get to know my kids' teachers, but not for the reasons that I have had to, because of diabetes.

These people will be more important in my child's life than they are for most children. Joel's health and safety will be in their hands in a much more immediate way than is true for a healthy child. Their cooperation, or lack thereof, makes a big difference in how smoothly things go for Joel at school. It also has a great impact for my husband and me as parents. If your school nurse, principal and teachers are already educated about diabetes and aware of what is required to manage it daily, you and your child are very fortunate. If you find that the school personnel don't seem to understand the things that need to be done for your child, it may be that you need to educate them or enlist others to help you to educate them. As I mentioned earlier about family and friends, it may be that they are not educated about diabetes and have never had experience with some-one who has it. Don't be as naïve as I was, thinking that the school principal or administrators are required to provide mandatory diabetes training for those teachers who have Joel in their classes. Even if there is another diabetic child in the school that may never be considered. The extent of a principal's involvement in making the staff and children at the school aware of diabetes may be very min-imal. It will likely be up to you to insist on more if that is what you want or feel is needed. In addition to your multiple, newly-acquired roles, make sure you add "diabetes advocate at school" to the list.

In many cases, nothing will be done to educate anyone at school that isn't initi-ated and carried out by you. Everything that is done to educate anyone at school may be done only at your request, if not insistence. From my experience with other parents and what I have been told by diabetes educators this is typical. If this is the case in your child's school it will be up to YOU to educate them. If you want things to change for your child and the staff at his school, you will most likely have to make those changes yourself. It isn't fair or easy but it is well worth it. You will have an amazing sense of accomplishment knowing that you have been the impetus for positive change for your own child and others who will follow him.

I have talked to a lot of parents about school nurses. There is a huge range of what is out there in elementary and middle schools today in staffing for school nurses. I have been amazed to learn that many elementary schools do not have full-time school nurses. Many school districts "share" one nurse between several buildings. While this is an unavoidable reality due to limited funding, it seems terribly dangerous for students with chronic illnesses such as diabetes. We feel fortunate that our school has a full-time nurse.

There is also disparity in the education of school nurses about diabetes. Some were trained in the day when you just deprived diabetics of all sugar. You and your school nurse may have different ideas of what is okay for your child to eat. Just as it is for parents, it is a fine line for school nurses between what is protective enough in regards to a child with diabetes and what is TOO protective. You will need to determine where this line is for you, your child and your school nurse. You and your school nurse will need to work together to determine what is reasonable for all of you.

Other school nurses may have had more current training but have had no practical experience at all with diabetes in the school setting. Perhaps your child is the only student in the school with diabetes and the nurse's previous experience has not allowed him or her opportunity to care for a child with diabetes. This may be difficult for both of you at first, but it may end up being a good thing because hopefully you can show her how you care for ***your*** child's diabetic needs specifically, and this will impact how she cares for your child at school. Every diabetic child is different, and you and she will have to develop a balance and working relationship with each other.

Still other school nurses manage to be both knowledgeable and practical about how to treat your child and you will feel so lucky that she is in your child's school. The bottom line is that you will have to make the best of what you get. Like it or not, this is the person you will be dealing with on a daily basis to help you care for your child. Obviously that will be a lot easier if you are on friendly terms with her. It is great if you can start out on the right foot with the school nurse. Just remember that it is unlikely that you will always see eye to eye about how to treat your child. If you can deal with these differences calmly as they come up you will both be much better off, and your child will know that everyone is working together to care for him.

Of course, this isn't always easy. These are the times when it will help to talk to another parent of a child with diabetes about working together with the school nurse to reassure yourself that your view is reasonable, even if your school nurse disagrees. Another parent of a child with diabetes understands both being the parent in charge AND how closely you must work with the school nurse. Most of your other friends won't get it. I am lucky enough to have a friend who gets it even though her child does not have diabetes. She spends so much time with Joel that even though her child does not have diabetes, she really knows what is involved.

You will need to work together with the nurse and staff at school to develop a system that you can all live with to care for your child while he is at school. Something I found that was very hard to understand as a newly diagnosed parent: we expected the school nurse to know all about diabetes because she is a nurse, and this is not necessarily the case. Even though she was trained to care for someone with diabetes that doesn't mean she has had current practical experience doing so. Knowing the target blood sugar range for a child is one thing. Helping him regulate and maintain blood sugars in that range on a daily basis is quite another. This is not to suggest that each of our school nurses are not qualified nurses, but rather that we all have to go through the same trial and error that all parents and medical professionals do. Unfortunately, this process defines diabetes management. As a newly diagnosed family, this is very difficult to accept from any medical professional. We want our child regulated and we want it now. Unfortunately, we all have to go through this trial and error process.

You and the school nurse may be doing more learning together about the specifics of your child's diabetes than you as a parent had envisioned. This does not mean that she doesn't know how to keep your child safe, although it may feel that way. But doesn't it also feel that way for you at home some days? Again, we are back to talking about the nature of the disease itself. The process of balancing doses of insulin and ratios of carbs is different for every diabetic. A variety of factors effect a child's blood sugar differently, and it will take time for both of you to learn what effects your child's blood sugar, and in what way. It may require some patience on your part to get used to the routine at school. And it is very difficult not to be there. You would like it all to be automatic, but it just can't be.

Our school nurse cares a great deal for Joel but we have certainly had our differences of opinion over how he should be treated. I have never doubted Joel's safety while he is under her care, which is of course the most important thing. We are very lucky to have someone who cares about Joel as much as Joel's school nurse. Knowing that your school nurse has an emotional connection to your child makes you feel reassured that she is really keeping an eye on him the way that you would.

Keep in mind that you are in charge of your child's diabetes care. This is not something that your child's school is going to go out of its way to point out to you, so know your own rights as a parent. You have so little control over most aspects of this disease; make sure you maintain control over this one. If you feel it is not in your control, you need to speak with your school nurse, and perhaps other school officials to work something out so that it is. Your child's doctor or nurse can be a great advocate for you in this way. Kathy has come to my defense on more than one occasion, and if nothing else, it reassures me that what I am doing for Joel is reasonable.

It is very easy to get caught up in the feeling that if you are not a nurse or doctor you must defer to their judgment. Once you have a basic working knowledge of diabetes you will be stunned by how capable you are of making major decisions about your child's diabetes care regimen. Needing to provide the school nurse with written medical orders from his doctor for every situation may make you feel less in control than you would like, but try to keep in mind that this fulfills a legal requirement for the nurse and the school, not one that questions your competence as a parent.

You will also need a communication system to go back and forth between school and home to communicate blood sugars and other important information with the school nurse. We have a notebook that goes back and forth between school and home each day to record Joel's blood sugars, insulin doses and carb counts for his lunch. This way we can all see how his blood sugars were during the day and get some idea of how his lunch and snacks affected his blood sugar. It is also necessary to provide carb counts for the nurse to assist Joel in calculating his bolus (insulin dose through his pump).

You will need to supply the school nurse with all medical supplies that your child will need including testing supplies, meter, glucagon, glucose tabs, pump supplies if the child is on a pump, syringes, snacks, juices, etc. Most likely his supplies will be kept in a designated area in her office. Joel's school nurse likes to have Joel's emergency glucagon kit in a fanny pack so that she can quickly grab it on her way out of the building for fire drills and other emergency evacuations. I strongly suggest that you do the same at your child's school even if your school nurse has not requested that you provide one.

The school principal is also a key player in your child's safety and comfort level in school. Again, some parents get lucky in this area and some don't. If you are lucky enough to get a principal who thinks progressively you may be able to do things like hold staff in-services to educate about diabetes, hold school assemblies to provide diabetes education to the entire school, hold diabetes walks or fundraisers, and review safety procedures with faculty. For the rest of us, we always have each other to complain to. One principal I have dealt with just didn't seem to get it. He seemed disinterested in what role he might play (if any) in making a diabetic child safer at school or what could be done to educate other students or teachers.

I have felt that a principal's presence or absence at key meetings or in-services is a pretty good indicator of whether he understands the gravity and responsibility of having a diabetic child at his school. His presence at such key meetings may not be required, but it may indicate to you his level of interest and involvement. If he or she is unable to attend a meeting and also doesn't follow up with you to see if you have any concerns, you get a very clear picture of where you stand. You cannot assume that the principal is overseeing your child's diabetic care. This does not happen automatically by any means. Remember, many people do not realize that diabetes is a life-threatening condition. With the recent publicity in the drastic rise in the number of cases of type 2 diabetes being found in children, many people make the mistake of thinking that this is the diabetes we are talking about.

Again, you are stuck with what you get but there are ways to make the best of it. One way to make a change in the education of the staff is to approach the school principal about offering a diabetes in-service training for the staff. This is assuming that he sees the need and value of educating his staff about diabetes. This may not be as obvious a conclusion for him to reach as it should be. If he does not see things as you do in terms of what kind of training needs to be done for the school staff and what steps should be taken to ensure your child's safety, another way to accomplish this is through establishing a 504 Plan, or Individual Education Plan, for your child. If the plan you write requires an educational in-service, the school will have to comply. This seems like a lot of formal effort to accomplish something that is just common sense to have done in the first place, and that is exactly what it is. But again, it will most likely be solely your responsibility to advocate for your child at school. Having this plan in place assures that certain things happen each year because the school's federal funding is dependent on the school following the 504 Plans.

This year we have put a 504 Plan in place for Joel which requires the school to do certain things regarding diabetes care and education. Among other things it requires a staff in-service taught by Joel's nurse at the Joslin Center. It also spells out what is expected; including not depriving him of special snacks (as Kathy says, treat him like a kid first and treat the blood sugar second; you can always correct it later), how and where he may test his blood sugar, safety measures for him while he travels on the bus, what he needs to do on physical education days to ensure his safety, and much more.

The 504 Plan falls under section 504 of the Rehabilitation Act of 1973. Another important law that pertains to children with diabetes is the Americans with Disabilities Act of 1990. Some parents disagree with diabetes being classified as a disability. Obviously, this is an issue each family has to explore for itself. For my husband and me there could not be a single issue more important than Joel's safety. We feel that the "label" of disability fades in comparison to the bigger and always more important issue of his safety. A 504 Plan ensures that the criteria in it will be carried out because the school's failure to do so threatens their federal funding. As much as we would all like to believe that everything reasonable will be done for our children in school to keep them safe and included as "typical" kids, this won't always happen on its own. The formal mandate makes it happen.

Just because your child has a fantastic teacher this year does not guarantee that will always be the case. The 504 Plan puts things in place so that they happen consistently regardless of your child's teacher, nurse or principal. For more information on 504 Plans visit the Children With Diabetes website at www.childrenwithdiabetes.com. The website has a sample plan for each grade level and it distinguishes between a plan for a child who is on shots and one who is on a pump. This website is a phenomenal resource for multiple issues related to parenting a child with diabetes.

If there is one area where I can really say we have been fortunate it is with the teachers Joel has had since he was diagnosed. I have already made reference to the wonderful Mrs. Musengo, the teacher he had the year he was diagnosed. Her level of understanding of diabetes was very high since her father had the disease, which made things so much easier for us. But our satisfaction with her as a teacher had much more to do with how she treated Joel. She was always aware of how he looked and if he seemed to be feeling OK. She was sensitive to his need to test a little more frequently when he felt unsure and she was so tolerant of this. She had an amazing knack for making him feel like a regular kid while still keeping a special eye out for him. As I said earlier, I never had a doubt that he was safe in her care.

Most schools in our area do not allow you to request a certain teacher at the end of the school year for the following year. My advice on this would be to respect this policy but to still look out for your child's special needs. Go right to the teacher your child currently has near the end of the school year (I do so in April). The class placement decision is generally in the current teacher's hands. I don't request a teacher by name but I let Joel's current teacher know what traits I am looking for and what traits I don't think would be suitable in a teacher for Joel. For example, most of us would not want someone who is not attentive or observant. Beyond that, patience and experience with other children with special medical needs is basically what I look for in a teacher. It is also very helpful if you have a teacher who is open to frequent communication with parents. I always tell his current teacher that my first priority is a teacher who can keep Joel safe. The academics will fall into place later; he is a strong student. Just give me someone who can keep him safe, which I feel translates into someone who pays close attention and has good common sense. Hopefully this includes all teachers but we all know that some are better than others. I have been so happy with his past teachers that I go to them, tell them what I am looking for and trust their judgment from there.

That is what I did with Mrs. Musengo and she didn't disappoint me. She put Joel in Mrs. Strobeck's 3rd grade class. Mrs. Strobeck had a son who had grown up with kidney disease and had a kidney transplant. She had a keen understanding of what it meant to have a child with a serious medical condition. She was patient and understanding but never hesitated to let me know if there was a problem with him testing too often or if he was having trouble in class. Joel thrived in her class as well.

At the end of this past school year I went to Mrs. Strobeck and made the same request: "Please put him in a class with a teacher who will do well with the added challenge of his diabetes." My first impression of Mr. James was that I could believe all the wonderful things I had heard about him. He has been perhaps the most open of all Joel's teachers so far about wanting to learn as much about diabetes as possible. He has been put in a position where more is expected of him because Joel is now testing his blood sugar in class, and he has certainly risen to the occasion. I believe that it takes a truly exceptional teacher to foster this kind of growth in a child, despite his own fears or hesitations about everything medical. Mr. James is just such a teacher. He has also allowed Joel himself to educate him about diabetes, which builds Joel's confidence even more.

You would think it would be scary for a 9 year-old to feel like he knows more about diabetes than his teacher, but I think for Joel it all goes back to *who is in charge of this disease*. There is no question that that person is Joel. Without sounding too much like a typical mother who thinks that her child is way ahead of every other child, in this area that happens to be true. He is exceptionally capable and responsible for a 9 year-old and his diabetes care is just one more thing he is really good at.

This year we have transitioned to having Joel test his blood sugar in the classroom. This kind of transition takes a lot of preparation and time, and it requires more direct participation and understanding on the teacher's part. Prior to implementing Joel's independent testing in the classroom, I know that most of the faculty and administration at his school probably thought we were nuts to think that Joel could take on such an enormous amount of responsibility for his own medical care. We have done so in baby steps, allowing him to show what he can do each step of the way while making sure it was done with safeguards in place. We have sat back and let Joel show them just what he can do. We believe they have been in complete awe of his confidence and abilities.

Joel is now at the stage where he does all of his own blood tests in the classroom and consults the nurse only when he needs to treat a high or a low. Rather than walking down to her office numerous times a day as he had to in the past, now almost everything can be done by phone from the classroom. This means he is missing less class time. It also makes him less dependent on the school nurse for management of his diabetes. If this is a transition you hope to make for your own child, expect it to take place over the course of a school year. With liability issues and what is typically done at a certain grade level in mind, the school will have a huge say in how much can be done independently and how quickly.

Just a note about school field trips: I hate them. Depending on the school district's past policies, you may be told that you HAVE TO GO on all field trips or your diabetic child will be left back at school while the rest of his class goes on the field trip. This is illegal. Your child's right to go on a field trip with an appointed staff member (instead of his parent) is protected by the Rehabilitation Act of 1973, the Americans with Disabilities Act of 1990, as well as the Individuals with Disabilities Education Act (IDEA). These may all be found in the National Institute of Health Publication. At the very least let school administrators know that you know these laws exist to protect your child.

By law the school district has to provide a nurse or qualified person to accompany your child on the field trip. They may come back to you with arguments that the district does not have enough staff or resources to provide a nurse to go on the field trip. In addition, the teachers' unions won't allow a teacher to take on the responsibility of emergency medical care. Both actually are reasonable arguments until you realize that it results in discrimination against a diabetic child just the same. You have to pick your battles. This battle I would choose to fight because it is worth fighting. It will make a difference to the next parent who has to face all of these school issues when they are possibly completely shell-shocked after just learning that their child has diabetes.

Let your local Joslin Center or medical professional fight the battle with you if you end up needing to. They are used to it and are really good at dealing with school administrators. Try to remember the main objective is to make your child's field trip experience as normal as possible if you do have to go along. This of course is much easier if your child is in elementary school rather than middle school or high school.

While I am on the subject of having a local Joslin Center, I have to comment on how lucky we feel we are to have one only 20 minutes away. It wasn't until I wrote this book that I discovered that there are only 23 in the entire country. I have never doubted the excellent care we get at our pediatrician's office, but diabetes is a specialty. I will not even address the obvious medical advantages of taking your child to a Joslin Diabetes Center because I feel they go without saying. Your average doctor or pediatrician is also not going to have experience in dealing with the additional issues that come up in school because of diabetes, school field trips, dealing with teachers, nurses, and principals and any other issues with which you may need assistance or advocacy. I truly feel that if we weren't living near one, we would move to an area where there was one. I include this only as something to think about, because I feel that without having experienced the medical care of a Joslin Center, you would have no way to know what you and your child could be missing.

In closing, I would like to add that it is always going to be easier for you and your child if there was a parent who preceded you who has already dealt with the school regarding the "diabetes issues" in your child's school. This may or may not be the case. You may find yourself in a school where they just don't know much about what needs to be done to ensure the safety of a student with diabetes because they have never had a student with diabetes in their school. That doesn't mean that they don't care about keeping your child safe. It means that you will need to take the time to work with them and teach them what they need to know. If this is the case, it is your job to do that. If you don't like the way things are being done, it will be your job to change it. And if you want ground-breaking protocol in place for your child's diabetes care at school, you just may have to break that ground yourself.

4

Taking Diabetes to School

There are few things in life that involve more preparation than sending a child with diabetes to school. This chapter serves as a checklist for what you need to do to prepare your child for a new school year. I am sure there will be something that I have forgotten, as I do each year when I do this for Joel. Since I am doing it right now in preparation for him to enter 4th grade in a week, let's hope I compile a complete list!

---

1. You will need to ask your child's doctor or nurse to write medical orders for school.

- They should provide the school nurse with your child's sliding scale correction chart as well as his insulin types and doses.
- They should include an extensive list of what to do in a variety of scenarios. For example: if he is high and is on his way to PE…If he is low and it is time to get on the bus, etc.
- In this day and age of litigation, most schools require written permission to carry out anything that is considered a medical decision. Any changes you make to the original instructions given by your child's doctor will need to be signed by the doctor.

---

2. You will need to get a bin for diabetic supplies to be kept in the nurse's office. Stock that bin with:

- snacks and juices
- glucagon (check the expiration date)
- pump supplies and new batteries for the pump (if applicable)
- syringes, alcohol wipes, lancets
- glucose meter and batteries, the manual for the meter
- gel frosting or glucose tabs (to treat low blood sugars)
- a spare medic alert bracelet

---

3. You will need to provide a small notebook or other daily communication system to be used between you and your school nurse.

- Record all blood sugars taken while at school.
- Have your child record his morning blood sugar in the logbook so the nurse can see what his blood sugar was before getting on the bus.
- Record the number of carbs your child is eating for lunch that day (if he is on a pump) so that she can use that to determine the lunchtime bolus.
- The nurse can use this notebook to let you know when you need to send in more of each type of supply as well.

4. You will need to provide information to your child's new teacher about the basics of diabetes.

- Try to boil this down as much as possible. It is very difficult to do, as there is so much pertinent information.
- This should include the basics of blood sugars, what to do in an emergency and some idea of how your child handles his diabetes (Is he terribly nervous around a new teacher? Does he take charge of teaching new people what to do? etc).
- The teacher also should be given a small tube of frosting to keep in her desk in case of emergency. Make sure you also give him/her instructions on how and when to use it. Your school nurse may fight you on this and consider the frosting "medicine". I have been told that this cannot possibly hurt Joel, even if it is given at the wrong time, so I make sure I tell the teacher that too.
- I have attached what I am providing Joel's teacher with this year at the end of this chapter.

5. You will need to teach your child's teacher what signs to look for when catching a low or high blood sugar.

- Tell them to watch for changes in attention span, looking "out of it," changes in alertness, changes in coloring, sweating, needing to use the bathroom more often, etc.
- Make sure the teacher knows that sometimes the same symptoms are experienced during a low and a high blood sugar and the only way to know which you are dealing with is to test.

6. You will need to provide the nurse with a list of frequently eaten "birthday treats" and their carb counts.

- Most schools require that you bring in only pre-packaged foods when it is your child's birthday.
- Many items are purchased from a bakery or grocery store without nutritional information printed on the package. The nurse will need to know how much to bolus for a cupcake, donut holes, etc.

7. Don't forget to include the specials teachers, main office, religious education teacher, band instructor, bus driver, sports coaches and anyone else who sees your child during the day at or after school.

- I give each of these people the same folder of information **with Joel's photograph on the cover.**
- Under the photo, it says his name is and that he has type 1 diabetes, which is a life-threatening condition.
- On the cover it says that the instructions included in the folder are important to his immediate safety.
- On the cover it also says that the folder should be left out for any substitute teacher to see upon arrival to the class.
- Each folder includes a tube of frosting to be used in an emergency. You should also make sure that your school nurse remembers to display a medic alert sign in your child's classroom for any substitute teachers to make sure they go right to your child's folder upon subbing for your child's teacher.

8. This year I created a set of flashcards for Joel and his teachers to use as a reference.

- They are on brightly colored 3x5 cardstock held together with a ring to flip through the facts on things like when to test blood sugar, when he should and shouldn't bolus, when and how to treat a low blood sugar, what to do on gym days, what to do if he is high after lunch, carb counts for special treats that might be brought into the classroom and what to do about his blood sugar at dismissal time.
- It seemed to be much less overwhelming for Joel's new teacher in September to have all of this broken down into the very basics. Even though the final responsibility falls on Joel and the school nurse, his teacher really appreciated having this information.

Don't forget that the other important part of sending your child with diabetes to school is educating the other children and adults about what your child is doing and why. Taking the mystery out of diabetes will make your child far less different to the other kids (and teachers). Do this through educating them with books or games. There are several great children's books about diabetes that are appropriate to read aloud to an elementary school class. We started with *Taking Diabetes to School* when Joel was in 2nd grade. See the Children's Book list at the end of the book for more recommendations by Joel of books your child and his classmates may benefit from. You can also make things a little more fun as they get older with a diabetes trivia game. Make flash cards with true or false statements on them and see how much the kids and adults know. After answering a question correctly or incorrectly out loud, the kids are more likely to remember the fact. You may find that after the same kids have been in class with your child for a couple of years they become quite knowledgeable. It is a good idea to let the parents of the kids in class know that you did a presentation on diabetes in school. I have attached the simple note that I sent home with my son's classmates the day of the presentation this year to give you an idea of what I like to communicate to the parents. We have always been fortunate to have open minded teachers who want me to come in and teach the class about diabetes. Just in case we aren't always that lucky we put it right in Joel's 504 Plan that this is something that has to happen at the beginning of every school year. Like so many other things the 504 Plan guarantees that this will happen no matter what the preferences of the teacher might be.

The following table includes the information that I include in the folders that I provide to Joel's teachers, bus driver, religious education teacher, main office, etc.

DIABETES BASICS

** This table is not meant to be used for any child other than Joel and should not be construed as medical advice. Its purpose is simply to show what KIND of information should be provided to the school.

DIABETES BASICS
The idea is to keep Joel's blood sugar within a good range; for him that is from about 100-160. If he is lower than 80, he feels shaky and needs something to eat or a juice. If he is higher than 160, he needs to correct it by giving himself a bolus (dose of insulin) through his pump, which he does independently. As you will see by the list below, diabetes is a constant balancing act. When in doubt Joel is your best resource. He has been doing this almost completely independently for quite some time.

Several things affect his blood sugar such as physical activity, time of day, illness, stress, excitement, food and drinks (especially those high in carbohydrates).

Below is a copy of the guidelines that Joel will have at his desk and in the nurse's office. These are the basics for him managing his blood sugars in school:

ANY TIME:

Any time that he feels shaky AND is below 80 he should have a juice. The only exception to this is if he is on his way to lunch. In that case, he can either have half of a juice, or go right to lunch, depending on how he feels. If he has treated a low in the morning, he needs to retest prior to lunch. If he has treated a high by giving a bolus, he should not give another bolus for at least an hour and a half OTHER THAN TO COVER HIS FOOD AT LUNCH. In other words, you don't correct twice within an hour and a half for being high.

If it is after 9:30 am and he is above 200, he should correct based on the attached chart. If he has gym that day and he is testing within 2 hrs prior to gym, he should bolus .4 less than the chart indicates. In other words, if it is 9:30 am and he has gym at 10am and his blood sugar is high, he should bolus .4 LESS than that chart indicates.

GYM CLASS:

If he is going to gym, he should test prior to gym. If he is less than 180 but above 130, he should have a 15-20 carb snack and not bolus for it. If he is less than 130, he should have a juice and not bolus for it. If he is above 250, he should correct HALF of what the sliding scale chart says because he is on his way to gym.

LUNCH TIME

If he is on his way to lunch and tests below 100, he should bolus .4 less than the appropriate amount for the carbs he has eaten. Joel uses a ratio of 1 unit of insulin to 30 carbs of food and with the school nurse's help he determines the correct dose to give himself. When he is above 151 prior to lunch, he is to correct using the sliding scale prior to lunch. Each day he will test prior to lunch and report back to the nurse after he has eaten to have her supervise him as he determines and gives his bolus.

AFTER LUNCH:
If Joel tests and is above 200 within an hour and a half of when he gave his lunch bolus, he should bolus .4 less to correct the blood sugar (because some of the lunch bolus is still working).

TREATS:
For birthday party treats, Joel should eat the treat and bolus for the amount of carbs appropriately. If no nutritional info is listed, please use the following chart:

mini frosted cupcake: 10 carbs
full sized frosted cupcake: 25 carbs
5 donut holes: 15 carbs
ice cream cup: 15 carbs
frosted cookie (small): 15 carbs
frosted cookie (large): 20 carbs
unfrosted cookie (small): 10 carbs
unfrosted cookie (large) :15 carbs

Joel should never be excluded from having the treat or told to bring it home for later. If an error is made in carb counting, it can be easily corrected later. It is much more important that he be included and treated like his classmates than to have perfect blood sugar that day.

DISMISSAL:
If Joel is less than 120 prior to getting on the bus at dismissal, he should have a 15-20 carb snack with no bolus. If he is above 200 at this time, he should correct according to the sliding scale chart. Any time he is over 300 or under 80 at dismissal time, please call parent rather than sending him home on the bus. It will be determined by Joel, his parent and the nurse whether he will ride the bus or a parent will pick him up.

WHEN SHOULD JOEL TEST? AND WHAT TO DO ABOUT THAT NUMBER
Any time he feels shaky or funny
If he is below 80 but he feels fine, and he is not about to have a meal or snack, he should have a small (15-20 carb) snack
Feeling funny or shaky can also mean that his blood sugar is high!
If he is below 80 and feeling shaky, he should have a juice by itself (no snack) and he should be monitored for a few minutes.
He should test:
When he gets up in the morning
Before Lunch
Around 3:00 in the afternoon before getting on the bus
Before Gym or physical activity
Any time he feels shaky or funny
If he is high(above 200) follow sliding scale chart (attached) to know how much he should bolus (give dose of insulin through his pump) to correct his number if needed.
For a meal, have him bolus the proper amount based on the carbs he is eating. He should get 1 full unit of insulin for every 30 carbs. For example, if he ate a meal that had 55 carbs, he would bolus 1.8. If there is a question, we always round down the amount of the bolus to be safe.
Prior to exercise or during exercise (unless his blood sugar is already over 200) he should have a 15-20 carb snack before doing anything very physical (more than 20 minutes worth of exercise). If he has not had a snack prior to the exercise, you should have him take a break after 30 minutes to eat something. If activity continues for a long period, have him test after 1 hr of activity.

If in doubt, call us or ask Joel
(*the actual phone numbers have been deleted for privacy, but this gives you an idea of how I have set the list up*)

IMPORTANT DIABETES PHONE NUMBERS
Karen and Kevin (Home)
Karen (Cell)
Kevin (Cell)
If for some reason you could not reach us:
Joslin Center tell them it is an emergency for Kathy Bratt
Kathy Bratt...Joel's nurse (pager)
Joslin Emergency (use after hours or weekends) ***
***To use this number, you will need Joel's name, your name, Joel's date of birth (*list actual birth date in case it isn't you calling*), and his Dr. (Kathy Bratt) and the phone number at which they should call you
Pediatrician's Office
Office #1
Office #2
Emergency
Emergency Contacts who are allowed to pick Joel up at school:
List of friends and family members who are on the list of people who may pick Joel up at school along with their phone numbers would be here.

WHAT TO DO IN AN EMERGENCY
(Again, follow your own doctor's medical advice; this is just the list that we leave for babysitters or caregivers)
If Joel is shaky and under 80, have him sit down and drink a whole juice BY ITSELF (no snack with it). Make him sit a few minutes before he resumes his activity. He should test again to make sure his blood sugar is coming up in 15 minutes.
If Joel is shaky and not aware of what is going on enough to take in juice, squirt one whole small tube of frosting in his mouth. This CANNOT hurt him if done at the wrong time.
IF JOEL IS UNCONSCIOUS
Roll him onto his side and administer glucagon injection THEN call 911
When Joel's Blood Sugar is High
When Joel is HIGH, follow the attached chart to figure out his correction dose (bolus). He is not supposed to have more than one in an hour and a half. For example, if it is before 9am and he bolused his breakfast at 8:05, it is too soon to have him bolus again unless he is really high (over 300). See chart with questions.
If he is above 250, he should test his ketones. Ketone strips are in his kit of supplies in the nurse's office if he wants to test his urine for ketones, along with a meter to test ketones if he wants to test them by testing his blood. Either way is fine.
If he continues to be high after his correction (an hour to two later), there may be a problem with his site (where his pump goes into his body). If he continues to be high, please call us: Karen cell phone, Kevin cell phone. Joel's sugar being high could also indicate that he is getting sick.
When Joel's Blood Sugar is LOW

If Joel is LOW (below 80) and feeling shaky,
give him a whole juice by itself with nothing to eat.

If Joel is around 80 and does not feel shaky, he should have a 15-20 carb snack.

WAIT 15 minutes (I know this is hard), have him re-test every 15 minutes until he is above 80. He should come up above 80 after one juice. He should follow up the juice with a small snack (15 carbs) after he has waited 15 minutes, then re-test to make sure he is above 80. If for some reason he is not above 80, allow him to have a second juice after 20 minutes.

If Joel feels low or shaky and wants to go to the nurse to test rather than test at his desk, he should never go alone. Have another student or teacher's assistant walk him down to the nurse.

If he is out of it, do not try giving him juice, squirt an entire tube of the frosting into his mouth. Even if he does not need it at the time, this CANNOT harm him.

SIGNS THAT JOEL NEEDS MEDICAL ATTENTION
Feeling Shaky
Differences in his attention span/alertness
Becoming pale or disoriented
Sweatiness
Excessive thirst or need to use the bathroom

The following is the letter that I wrote to Joel's school principal near the end of the school year last year (around April). I began the process of requesting certain traits in a school teacher for the upcoming school year by sending this letter to both the principal as well as Joel's current teacher. I then asked that his teacher do her best to place Joel with the best teacher for his needs.

Dear School Administrator or Principal,

We would like to make our request for our son Joel's teacher for the 2005-2006 School Year when Joel will be entering the 4th Grade. Since Joel developed Type I Diabetes 18 months ago our number one concern has been his physical safety. As I am sure you can imagine, it is extremely difficult to have a child with a life-threatening chronic illness. It is even more difficult, once you have finally learned and established the best way to take care of him yourself, to trust his care to someone else. This is why the choice of his teacher is such an important one. This will not only influence how he does academically as it would for most children, but it will have a great impact on his physical health, well-being and confidence in his own ability to care for himself as well.

Pat Musengo could not have been more phenomenal in her dealing with Joel's diabetes. Joel was first diagnosed when he was in her class. After missing only 2 days of school he returned to find a warm, accepting teacher and classroom environment where they not only welcomed him back, but wanted to learn about his illness. Pat's amazing ability to make Joel feel both special and like every other kid is a true testament to her strengths as a teacher and as a human being. At the end of 2nd Grade I went to Pat, asking her to place Joel in a 3rd grade class where he would have the teacher who would best understand and be attentive to his needs. Gail Strobeck was just that person. Mrs. Strobeck has allowed Joel to teach her, as well as her class about what he needs to do to take care of himself. Mrs. Strobeck rose to the occasion each time there was a concern with Joel needing to test his blood sugar too often or being uncertain of how he was feeling, with her patience and understanding of the situation. Her personal experience with a child with a chronic medical condition allowed her to understand far better than most teachers ever could the specific challenges that both we and Joel face each day. She communicated with us openly each time there was a concern that needed our attention so we could work with Joel. We always know that she is paying attention to what is going on with Joel. She lets us know ahead of time when there will be a special treat in class so we can do what we need to do for him so that he may be included with the rest of the class without making him stand out as different at the time of the celebration. It is critical that he be treated like every other kid and included in "treat" celebrations in class.

In addition to the experiences mentioned above, Mrs. Musengo and Mrs. Strobeck both were very attentive to Joel, a critical part of knowing he is OK throughout the day. He could get into medical trouble very quickly and having a teacher who is keeping a close eye on him is very important. It is easy to mistake the symptoms a diabetic experiences with a low blood sugar for a child who is just sleepy or not paying attention. We also believe that their years of teaching experience played a very important role in how skilled they were at handling Joel's medical issues. **They each mastered the difficult task of being aware of Joel's needs without letting him be defined by them.**

These two amazing educators have gone far beyond our expectations of what Joel's teacher could offer him in terms of both his education and his medical needs. We have the same hopes for his 4th grade teacher, and we look to you and Mrs. Strobeck (and I would hope even Mrs. Musengo) to make this decision. Please keep in mind the following qualities when placing Joel in a 4th grade class: years of teaching experience (we prefer more years of experience), patience, attentiveness, confidence, reassuring, exposure to medical issues and the ability to pay attention to specific needs without setting him apart from other kids.

We thank you for your attention to this matter and hope that Joel's 4th Grade experience will be as positive as each of the previous years have been. I will be discussing this with Mrs. Strobeck as I am sure that she has a strong sense already of who the right teacher for Joel might be. Thank you again for your time and consideration.

Sincerely,

Karen Hargrave Kevin Hargrave

A Note to Parents of kids in Mr. James' Class,

Hi, my name is Karen Hargrave and my son Joel is in Mr. James' class with your child. Today my husband and I came into class to tell the class about Joel having Type I diabetes. Joel will need to test his blood frequently throughout the school day, and we have found in the past that it is easiest if the other kids understand what is going on with Joel from the beginning of the school year. It is also important for Joel's safety that the kids in his class know what to do if he ever needs help. Today they learned a lot of things about diabetes such as the following:

-You can't catch diabetes by playing with Joel or being his friend.
-Type 1 diabetes is a disease where the cells in your pancreas that produce insulin stop working, so you have to take insulin through a shot or an insulin pump instead.
-Joel tests his blood several times a day.
-If Joel is going to exercise, he needs to test his blood first and sometimes snack.
-If his blood sugar is low, he needs a snack or juice.
-If his blood sugar is high, he needs some insulin.
-Joel uses an insulin pump to deliver the amount of insulin his body needs.
-Joel has to use his pump every time he eats or drinks.
-You don't grow out of Juvenile(Type 1) Diabetes.
-You don't get it by eating too many sweets.
-If Joel doesn't look right, you need to tell the teacher right away.
-Joel doesn't want to be treated differently than anyone else.

If you would like to take a moment to talk to your child about what he/she learned today that would be great. A wonderful source for more information is the Children with Diabetes Website. Go to: www.childrenwithdiabetes.com
If your child is particularly interested in books for kids about diabetes, we have let Mr. James borrow some of our favorites for the class for the remainder of the month.

Please feel free to call us with any questions or concerns that you might have (*list phone number*).

Thank you,
Karen, Kevin and Joel Hargrave

PART III

Getting Support

5

Taking Care of You

It may seem odd that at such an early point in this book I am making it about YOU. Somehow, I think if you are reading this book because you are the parent of a child with diabetes, you know why. Just when everything has become about your child and his diabetes you realize that you are at your breaking point. How can you possibly get a break from all of this intensive caregiving? And even more importantly, how can you admit to others that you are feeling "selfish" and need a break?

If you are someone who is not good at asking for help, you are going to have to get over it. You are going to need help. If your child is newly diagnosed, the prospect of leaving him with someone else is terrifying. It just seems easier not to go out or do things for yourself for awhile. In the long run you are only hurting your child and yourself if this is the approach you take. This is only my opinion of course, but allow me to attempt to persuade you if you don't already agree. Caring for a child with diabetes is an emotionally and physically exhausting, 24/7 job. You would not trust a nurse or doctor who never rested to care for you or your child. Why should you be any different?

You are also teaching your child a few things if you never take a break:

1. They are so fragile that no one but you can care for them.
2. You will always have to be with them in order for them to be safe.
3. They have nothing to contribute to their own diabetes care.

This last one is obviously somewhat dependent on the child's age but I have heard parents report that a child as young as 19 months can indicate when they feel a low blood sugar. If they learn from an early age that THEY are an important part of keeping their diabetes regulated, the transition to adulthood and taking care of their own diabetes will be that much easier.

Aside from your child's perceptions, you need and deserve the break. All parents do. When you add the care of a diabetic child to the demands of "typical" parenting, I doubt you could find anyone who would not advocate you getting a break. It will also be incredibly rejuvenating for you to get out, get away and get a break from diabetes for awhile. Don't feel that you don't deserve a break from it just because your child can't have one. Chances are that your child is not awake at night worrying about his A1C, heart disease and kidney failure like you are. It is also good for you to see that someone else can care for your child successfully without incident.

Don't rely on someone else to recognize your need to get away from diabetes. If I am guilty of anything, it is appearing that I have it all together and I'm doing okay. I complain to my friend frequently that it is the "together" person who never gets offered help. It is not because people don't care; it is because you don't obviously NEED help as desperately as someone who is going around crying all day, can't get anything done and can't remember where she left her car keys. Be your own advocate and don't be afraid to speak up about needing help and needing to get away.

Where do you find someone who can care for your child? I understand that this is a very scary question to ask. You feel almost negligent as a parent to even be thinking about it. Consider these possibilities:

1. **Close family members**. Chances are they spend a lot of time with you and your child already so it will be easier for them to pick up on the diabetes routine. They may feel unable to do it at first but didn't you? Give them a chance and reassure them that you don't expect them to go solo at first. Let them practice being in charge when you are still there with them if they have questions.
2. **Close friends**. What about the friends your child already has play dates with? Are you close to their parents? Or at least comfortable enough to ask them if they would assume the responsibility if you taught them about the diabetes care your child needs? Your adult friends are another great option. You may be surprised by how much responsibility they are willing to take on, but you have to ask.
3. **Nursing students** or other college students. Do you live close to a college or university? How about a hospital with a nursing program? Con-

sider inquiring about a nursing student as a babysitter. Think of the great practice she will get!

4. **Older kids with diabetes**. This may sound funny, but who would know better than someone who lives the disease themselves? If you are unsure about how to make these connections, approach your doctor or endocrinologist. Because of confidentiality they won't be able to give you names, but maybe you could post a flyer at their office.
5. **Other parents who have children with diabetes**. You may be able to strike up a great deal trading nights out. And even if your child's routine is different from theirs, you wouldn't need to teach them nearly as much as someone who doesn't live with diabetes.
6. **Neighbors.** It is a lot easier for a teenage babysitter to be comfortable with an extra medical issue like diabetes if the babysitter's own Mom and Dad are right across the street. Our babysitter Matt is a wonderful and capable person but diabetes is a lot of responsibility for anyone. Having his parents right across the street in an emergency makes a difference. If you aren't sure you are comfortable with this try isolating yourself in a room of the house the first few times to let them practice with the safety net of you being home. You should also ask the parents first if it is OK for their child to assume this kind of responsibility. A lot of parents may not want the liability of their child being in charge of a child with diabetes.

What else can you do to take care of yourself?

- Take a long bubble bath.
- Call a friend who is supportive and fun.
- Read a book.
- Take a walk.
- Watch a good movie on TV.
- Write in a journal.
- Keep a scrapbook.
- Write a letter to a friend.

- Look into locating and joining a support group in your area for parents of children with diabetes. If there isn't one, start one!
- Take up a hobby you have wanted to try, even though you probably don't have a lot of time.
- Set a time aside each week to do something you enjoy.
- Make a list of all the things you are proud of about your child who has diabetes. Now make a list of things you are proud of about yourself.
- Surround yourself with positive people.
- Surround yourself with friends who care about you and want to understand your child's diabetes.

On a personal note, I have to add that my "Diabetes Scrapbook" that I started working on in the days after Joel was diagnosed was the most therapeutic thing that I could have done for myself in those first weeks. Maybe I was just thrilled to finally be using my Art Therapy training even if only on myself, or maybe it was just a great distraction from giving shots and recording blood sugars. But it was so helpful to write about what we were going through, to record those early days, to take pictures of Joel going back to school and testing the first time at school and to save the cards and e-mails from family and friends. Most of all, it was important to embrace the fact that, like it or not, this was going to be a permanent part of Joel's life so I might as well record it in a scrapbook like I do with every other part of my family's lives. I am now into my 2nd large scrapbook dedicated to Joel's diabetes and it is great to be able to look back at where we have been through pictures of diabetes camps, pump training, diabetes walks and Family Diabetes Education Weekends.

Getting back to what you can do for you, try to be creative and do something that appeals to you and that you enjoy. When you want to splurge a little, try something from this list:

- Get a manicure or pedicure.
- Go to the movies with a friend.
- Go window shopping with a friend.
- Go for coffee or dessert with a friend.
- Buy a new CD and enjoy listening to it.

- Subscribe to a magazine that interests you.
- Go to your favorite store when you don't need anything; just enjoy looking to relax.
- Take a whole day (or a half day) to do whatever you want.

These things may seem small but they will make a difference if you are doing something for yourself on a regular basis. Don't let anyone make you feel guilty for taking time for yourself. You need it!

6

Supporting Your Friend Who is a Parent of a Child with Diabetes

I almost just asked my friend Maggie to write this chapter. She easily could; she is an incredible support for me. She always seems to know what to ask, when to ask it and when to just shut up and be there. I think that there are days I would have gone crazy without her. I am sure that she gets very sick of hearing about diabetes but I have never gotten that feeling from her. Let me give you some examples of things that Maggie has done to make me feel that she is an amazingly supportive friend.

- She, her husband, and her daughter (who is Joel's best friend) walk with us every year for our local diabetes walk. This year they even did their own fundraising letter requesting donations to mail out to their friends and family.
- She learned what she needed to know to take on the responsibility of having Joel over to play without me being there.
- She suggested that we have a sleep over with the kids so I could show her how to test Joel's blood sugar at night. That way she could watch him for us overnight sometime so Kevin and I could get away.
- She, her husband and her daughter attended our local JDRF Gala Auction and purchased a puppy named Rufus and they kept his name. For anyone who doesn't know, Rufus is the name of the teddy bear that is given to children who are newly diagnosed with diabetes. There is also a children's story about him, *Rufus Comes Home.*
- She is voluntarily attending the in-service given at Joel's school this week to train his teachers and school staff about diabetes so that she may be more knowledgeable when she baby-sits for Joel.

- She learned how to do a site-change and did one so that I would have another person to count on in a pinch.

I could go on but I think you get the point. The best thing that each parent with a child with diabetes could do for themselves is to find a friend like Maggie. I realize this is a very difficult task; she is the best.

I think that this chapter is helpful for people who are NOT the parent of a child with diabetes, but perhaps have a niece or a nephew with diabetes, or a good friend or neighbor who has a child with diabetes. If you are the parent of a child with diabetes, consider loaning this book to a friend of yours when you are done, as you thank her for being there for you in such an important way. Point out this chapter as one that might be particularly helpful to her. You can also offer it to a friend as a suggestion of what is helpful to you.

I think the best thing you can do for someone who is parenting a child with diabetes is be there to listen. That sounds so easy but I am sure it is not. There are ways to do this that are much more helpful than others.

How to be there for a friend who has a child with diabetes:

1. **Ask how our child is before we have to bring it up**. A lot of the things we do for our child are just a plain pain in the neck. A lot of the time, we ARE complaining. But at other times, we are just stating the aspects of the daily routine. If you ask about Joel I won't feel like I'm complaining or running on and on. As a parent of a diabetic child you never quite know how much you should say and what is too much information. This is even hard with your close friends. Your questions let me know that you care and want to listen.

2. **Try to be one of the people who gets it.** There are certain friends and family members who you can tell right away have no understanding of what you are going through and they may not ever. I try really hard not to hold that against them, but at the same time, I want people to understand what we are all going through.

3. **Ask us how our child is doing.** It is really nice when someone asks you because you don't feel like you are burdening them; you are just answering their question.

4. **Don't zone out when we talk about the medical stuff.** Even if you don't follow everything we are saying, ask questions so you understand it. We like to explain it. It makes us realize that you are actually listening! It also reinforces my sense of my own competence. Remember, we didn't understand it all right away either. It is impossible to talk about what we are going through without talking about the medical stuff, it is all medical stuff. I have a sister-in-law, Sandie, who is a nurse and she also has type 2 diabetes. I can always talk about the medical stuff with her. She gets it and she never gets sick of listening or talking about it. That is a great break for me when I just need to talk about it without having to give an explanation of medical terms and concepts first.

5. **Don't gloss over things when we need to talk** by saying something like, "Is everything stable? Has he evened out yet?" Both of these statements sound like you mean that his blood sugar is not fluctuating and that just shows that you have no understanding of the disease. Diabetes is all about the ups and downs of blood sugar. The fluctuating up and down is the nature of the disease. It doesn't stabilize or even out. A child's blood sugar that is up and down is not "out of control." A child whose blood sugar goes up and down has diabetes! Statements like these seem to be made by people who like it when everything is running smoothly and they seem to think that by phrasing their question in that way. they are asking you to say, "Yes, everything is just fine." The truth is that my child's blood sugar may be very up and down and everything is still fine. Everything running smoothly doesn't always happen with diabetes, and when people pretend that it does it minimizes the very real feelings of helplessness we parents have. We like when everything goes smoothly too, but most of the time, despite our greatest efforts and knowledge, they don't go smoothly. When someone asks me that it feels like they are implying that there is something more that I could be doing to make things better. I already have a child with a life-threatening illness; I don't need any more guilt over what I am not doing to help him.

6. **Don't be afraid to ask serious questions about health complications**. Most parents will be grateful for your interest. It is the rare friend who can show that kind of forthright concern. It is my nature to deal with things out in the open; just ask any one of my friends. I really feel that this is what most parents in our situation would prefer. It seems, however, to be quite taboo for someone to ask if your child will have any long term health complications. I guess a lot of people are concerned that they will upset us by bringing

up the subject of major health problems. It isn't as though we haven't already read and obsessed over every possible health complication from diabetes. You are not going to put a new idea into our heads by asking about it. It is much worse to have it go without being said at all. I often wonder what gets said behind my back by those family members and friends who are afraid to ask those questions of me directly. I am sure that they have some of the same misconceptions about diabetes that I did before I asked the nurse about them. From my interpretations of the actions of others on my most emotional days, I have felt that when people don't ask, they either don't care or are unaware of the major health risks that are very real for Joel. Deep down, I know that this is probably not the case, but it is an easy conclusion to jump to when your emotions are taking over.

7. **Let your children get involved with the child who has diabetes.** I think it would be rare in this day and age to find someone who would actually exclude someone from their group of friends for having diabetes, but you never know. Kids may have a tendency to stay away from things they don't understand. Imagine how afraid your child will be to play with a child who has diabetes if you are afraid to ask questions about the disease or talk about it openly with your child. Don't just gloss over the fact that your child's friend or classmate has diabetes. Don't make it the elephant in the room that no one can talk about. Just as I talk to the kids in my son's class each year you should talk about diabetes and the real facts openly with your children, especially if the child with diabetes is a good friend, family member or neighbor. Your child may have real concerns about the child for the short and the long term. They also may have myths built up in their own minds that are totally untrue. As their parent it is your job to clear those myths up. One of Joel's friends was worried that Joel could only be safe if I stayed with him all the time and she got a little nervous when I was not there. Her mother explained to her that Joel knew what to do to take care of himself, and so did she. Another friend thought that Joel could not do any exercise when he came over to play at his house. His mother quickly asked him, "Doesn't Joel play during playtime at school and in gym class?" Once the boy realized that this was true he relaxed about what Joel could do when he came over to play. Education is the key for children, just as it is for adults.

8. **Don't ignore the diabetes or whisper about it to your child like it is something that has to be hush-hush with the diabetic child in the room.** Sometimes a well-intentioned family member or friend may do this in an

effort not to make the diabetic child feel different. It doesn't work that way. No one likes to be ignored or whispered about. They are different and ignoring the fact that they are testing their blood sugar right in front of you may make them feel like they should be embarrassed by needing to do it. Comment on what they are doing or ask a question. Make sure that the other kids understand what they are doing and why they are doing it, and make sure that they know it is OK to ask questions too. I have never seen Joel get upset by a question someone asked. He has, however, asked if certain people know about his diabetes because they never ask or talk about it. Remember that it is a huge part of his life. How could someone not talk about it or acknowledge it?

9. **Learn what to do if a diabetic child or adult is in trouble, then teach your child**. It may be scary for a child who doesn't live with diabetes daily but it will be far scarier if an emergency happens and they don't know what to do. Depending on your child's age, tell them to always be aware of how the diabetic child looks and is acting. Tell them if he ever starts to act funny, slurs words, seems sleepy, shaky, etc., to get an adult immediately. Since I have no medical background (other than motherhood), it is not appropriate for me to tell you what to do in a medical emergency. It is appropriate for you to ask the parent of the diabetic child you know or a doctor what to do, practice it and become comfortable doing it.

7

Family Diabetes Education

One of the best things our family has done for Joel and our whole family since he was diagnosed with diabetes, is to attend a Diabetes Family Education Weekend. At our first Family Diabetes Education Weekend we got some information about Joel's care, but we also met other people who were going through the same thing we were. My husband and I met other parents, Joel met other children with diabetes, Casey met other siblings and my Mom met other grandparents. In this group we were not the family who stuck out because their child has diabetes. All of the families had diabetes, and all the families got to see how other families were getting through it. We went to the weekend expecting to get educated by the organization and presenters running the weekend. We left the weekend having gotten even more from the other parents attending the weekend.

There is something to be said for how much it helps to be around other people who are in the same situation as you. You don't have to explain how isolating diabetes feels; they know. You don't have to tell them how scary it is in the middle of the night when your child's blood sugar is too high or too low; they have been there. You don't need to tell them how unfair it is that your child got this terrible disease; they know that too. They feel that unfairness in a way your other friends can't because they live it too. They understand the pain you feel when you wonder what you did to cause or didn't do to prevent your child from getting diabetes. Even though you know it is not logical you think it. And chances are they have thought it too.

My friend Maggie (remember her, the one who gets it) described it so well for someone who doesn't live it every day. She said, "It is like always waiting for the other shoe to drop. That is the kind of heightened awareness that you have to have all the time." I describe it as the diabetes' way of reminding you that you don't get to relax the way most parents sometimes can (although rarely). Just when you let your guard down, there is a blood sugar of 450 and you panic until you figure out why and can get it back down. You finally schedule a day away for yourself and your child's pump site falls out and you are the only one he wants to fix it for him. The dreaded stomach bug pays a visit and you end up at the ER instead of just in the bathroom like every other parent. There are so many scenarios that could be listed here, but unfortunately, you know them all.

The parents who you meet at a Family Diabetes Education Weekend understand why you and your spouse haven't gone away alone together since your child was diagnosed. They know why you rarely, if ever, get to go out with your spouse. They know why you haven't slept through the night in months. They don't think it is weird that you use a baby monitor for your 9 year-old to make sure he isn't having a seizure during the night. They know what is involved with each new school year, as you have to educate a new teacher about the basics of diabetes. They know that you have the phone number of the school nurse programmed into your cell phone and memorized. They know that even though you seem like a big-mouthed militant Mom, you really just want your child to be included in all that he should be included in, while keeping him safe at the same time. Is that really so much to ask? They understand why you cringe when it is someone's birthday in your child's class and there will be cupcakes and you just have to hope he won't have unwanted attention drawn to him over whether or not he can have one.

You gain so much from talking to and being with these other parents. It was far more comforting than I ever had imagined. I got as much from the listening as I did from the talking. You can compare the good, the bad and the ugly about your child having diabetes. You can be open and honest about your feelings. No one is going to judge you for complaining there. Everyone at this weekend knows exactly why you are complaining and that you are entitled to complain! You will also get the chance to hear that you don't have the worst school nurse on the planet, that your child's diabetes could be worse or his health even more fragile than it is, you could have even bigger obstacles at your child's school or family members who are totally unwilling to help. If it is done well, you will also come away with a wealth of practical information that you will be using to care for your child.

To find out if there is a program in your area, do a search online or check with your local JDRF(Juvenile Diabetes Research Foundation) Chapter. Consider traveling to a program out of state if there is not one in your state. We travel to the SETEBAID (diabetes spelled backwards) program in Pennsylvania even though we live in New York, and each year we encounter people from all over the Northeast. It is well worth the trip and can be a fun getaway for your whole family. To give an example of some of the seminars you might find, I will list below some of the topics we have chosen from in the past.

Technological Advances
Insulin Pumps
Hypoglycemia
Using Glucagon
Working with Your School Nurse
Diabetes at School
Supporting Yourself and Getting Support
Babysitting Someone with Diabetes
Nutrition and Carb Counting

8

Diabetes Support Groups

You may already be saying, "I am not a support group kind of person." If you are, you owe it to yourself to try. I have found that there is a huge range of what people consider a support group and somewhere in that range may be the support group that is right for you. If you do not live in an area where family diabetes education weekends are offered, support groups may be your only way of finding other parents who are going through the same experiences you are going through. You can check in several places to find out if there is currently a support group offered in your area. Start at your local Juvenile Diabetes Research Foundation Chapter. But be prepared: if you show interest and they don't currently have a support group they may ask you to start one. This is not necessarily a bad thing. You may find that starting your own support group, or doing so with someone else, will really make you feel good. Not only will you be getting the support that you need, but you will be offering that same kind of support to someone else who needs it. You can also inquire about a support group at your local Joslin Center, endocrinologist's office or pediatrician's office. You can also look online for resources and information on support groups in your area. You may even want to consider an online support group.

Once you are involved in a support group or running your own group, there are several benefits you can expect as a member of such a group.

- You will feel less alone.
- Finally, you will be in a roomful of people who know what it is like to be raising a child with diabetes.
- You won't be spending 80% of the time you spend talking to them trying to explain what it is like.
- You can go straight to the issue at hand because they will already know what it is like.

- You will have numerous new resources for information and the practical aspects of raising a child with diabetes.
- You can turn to these other parents to find things out, such as which diabetes camp to take your child to, which doctors are the best in your area, how you deal with your school nurse, how they got their child to handle shots better or consider going on the pump, etc.
- At the same time you are getting the benefit of this information from these parents, they will be getting those same benefits from knowing you.

Even if you think you have nothing to share at this point, you do. Your experience with your child is unique and chances are many of the other parents can relate to it. When our son was first diagnosed, I certainly felt like I had nothing to offer the experienced parents, but I did. I made them feel like experienced parents. It helps to feel like you are helping someone else especially when you know what they are going through.

An additional benefit is that many support groups include the kids. In the group we attend through our local Joslin Center, the adults go in one room, and the kids go in another, with qualified medical staff so you don't need to worry about them. This gives both the parents and the kids the chance to gain support from their peers. The kids may already know each other from diabetes camps and other local events. If they begin to see many of the same kids at events, they are immediately more comfortable. The more time the parents spend together, the more comfortable they feel sharing such personal details of their lives. Even if you don't think a support group could be for you, don't make that decision until you have given it a try.

PART IV

Diabetes Sucks

9

Birthday Parties

It may seem odd that I am dedicating an entire chapter to birthday parties. This chapter is about much more than just birthday parties. How do you make sure it is safe for your diabetic child to go to something like a birthday party without making him stick out by being the only child whose parent stays for the party? How can you leave the additional responsibility of your child's diabetes with the parent who already has the responsibility of giving a birthday party for 10+ children? These questions plagued me for months after Joel was diagnosed with diabetes. I still don't know all the answers, but it has gotten easier to accept that sometimes there are no good answers and we do the best we can.

To me, birthday parties represent the hundreds of little things that are difficult for diabetic children and their parents. They represent the hundreds of things that parents of children who do not have diabetes would never think of as being an issue for us. Birthday parties, play dates, sleepovers, an afternoon at a friend's house, sports, bike rides down the block and dozens of other kids' activities that at a certain age usually become things that the child does independently become issues for the child with diabetes. When the parent whose home your child is visiting doesn't know anything about diabetes, this becomes even more complicated.

One of the first birthday parties Joel was invited to after he was diagnosed was a 3-hour outdoor sledding party on an isolated hill in the country with 25 other children invited. I called the Mom to tell her "we" would be coming, and then I said I hoped that she understood that I would need to stay because of his diabetes. Her dismissive response of, "Oh no, you can leave him, he'll be fine" was as ridiculous as it was well-intentioned. She just didn't get it. How could she? For some reason, as I stood outside freezing the afternoon of that birthday party, I became particularly upset by the level of normalcy that had been taken from Joel (and us) by his diabetes. I couldn't just drop him off like the other kids' Moms.

He couldn't just go anywhere, anytime, no matter whose parents were in charge. This would only get more difficult as he got older, and perhaps it was my anticipation of that which was particularly upsetting.

For those of you who are reading this and are not the parent of a child with diabetes, I realize that you may not know why leaving Joel alone at this birthday party was such an issue. Exercise effects a person's blood sugar dramatically. He can easily go very low OR very high depending on how the physical activity affects him that day. This can happen right away, hours later or the next morning. Joel typically needs a snack before he exercises and then needs additional snacks after 30-60 minutes of exercise. There is a lot of trial and error involved, and the testing and snacking has to continue during the exercise and for at least an hour AFTER the exercise is finished. You would not give these tasks to someone who doesn't do them on a regular basis, much less at a birthday party, outside in 20 degree weather with 25 kids sledding!

Here are some tips I have come up with to keep you from going crazy over birthday parties and those hundreds of other things like them that other parents just take for granted. If you have more tips please send them to ME; I need all that I can get too!

1. Make sure you have at least one friend who gets it, who you can talk and complain to.

2. Reach out to meet other parents of children who have diabetes, because you know that they will get it. Seek these parents out at diabetes support groups, online through the Children with Diabetes website, diabetes camps or Family Diabetes Education Weekends.

3. Attend Diabetes Family Education Weekends whenever and wherever they are available (more on this in Chapter 9). You may hear some great strategies to deal with this type of frustration that you had not thought of.

4. Make a deal with yourself to do something nice for yourself after you have spent an afternoon at a birthday party!

5. Make friends with the parents of your child's friends. It makes the time at those birthday parties and play dates go a lot faster. If your child tends to get invited to the same kids' parties every year (if you are lucky), these parents may eventually become educated enough about diabetes over time that you will become comfortable allowing your child to stay at the party without you.

6. Make a rule for your children (both the one(s) with diabetes and the one(s) who does not have diabetes) that they only attend parties and play dates of children they are actually good friends with. These days, the entire class frequently gets invited to birthday parties and it gets ridiculous and expensive to accept every invitation. If limiting attendance becomes your family's policy it is amazing how your children will start to understand that just because they get invited, it doesn't mean that they are going to the party.

7. If one of the other parents is one whom you trust, perhaps that parent would be willing to stay at one birthday party instead of you, just to give you a break, and make your child not always be the one who has his parent there. Of course, this all depends on how acceptable this plan is to both of your children. Assuming that you can work it out, this other parent, who will probably be a good friend of yours, could just serve as an extra set of eyes to watch over your child while the parent giving the party is likely too busy to do so. The parent could call you if there was any question about how much he needed to bolus or inject, etc.

8. Make sure your child(ren) know that if you are going to spend your afternoon at a birthday party with them, that may mean they will need to help you with some chores before you go. I find that it makes me less resentful of losing all of that time sitting at a birthday party if when I get home my "to do" list isn't a mile long. There is nothing wrong with teaching your child that you do chores before doing something fun.

9. Show up a little late to every party you go to (except for their very closest friends). It is amazing how much of a mental difference that little bit of time can make.

Many of the guidelines listed below can be applied to the other situations mentioned at the opening of this chapter such as play-dates and sleep-overs. Some common themes are the following:

1. **Your willingness and ability to ask for help.** This sounds a lot easier than it is. It is not easy for many of us to do for so many reasons. You may be a very self-sufficient person who doesn't like to admit that you need help. You also may not trust another parent to care for your child.

There are a lot of things to remember when caring for a child with diabetes. Many of them become second nature to us and you may forget to share important information with someone else who is going to watch your child. It is difficult to remember everything you need to share. **Write it down**. I finally compiled a notebook of information to be referenced by anyone who was taking care of Joel. It seems like a lot of work, and it is. But once you complete the work, you don't have to do it over and over. You also may feel as though you are burdening someone else with what you see as your responsibility. Maybe you are; that is what friends are for. And truly good friends do not see this as a burden. This is something you will have to work out in your own mind.

2. **You have to let your child know that there are limits to how much you can ask of another parent in a setting such as a birthday party.** This is a tough one because you are basically saying to your child, "This is just too much to ask." You feel so guilty admitting to your child that his diabetes is a burden. Try to avoid this particular pitfall. No one knows what a burden his diabetes is more than he does. Be open and honest with him about what you feel comfortable doing and asking of another parent. Problem-solve together with your child about possible ways you could handle it. It may be a work in progress for both of you.

3. **Your child is not going to go to every event he is invited to**. If your child goes to everything he is invited to, whether he is diabetic or not, he is probably over-scheduled like most of the children in this country, (but that is the subject for another book!) It is not a bad lesson for him to learn that he has to make choices and can't do it all. That has less to do with him having diabetes and more to do with keeping a balanced life.

As far as play dates go, my best suggestion is to have your child become friends with great kids who have great parents! This is not always easy or within your control, but it is by far the best way in my opinion to ensure his safety and your comfort level while he is away from home. I do not recommend you turning your child into the bubble boy and never letting him out of your sight. That only teaches him that he is fragile and that only you can care for him. I think most of us would agree that is not the message we want to send our children. On the other hand, finding parents with common sense and a willingness to take on the added component of diabetes at a play date is a real concern. Take the time to teach them the basics and you will help take much of the mystery out of the disease for them. Their being more comfortable will undoubtedly contribute to their willingness to have your child over to play.

10

What About the Siblings?

I really can't imagine how hard it is for our son Casey to deal with all of the attention his brother Joel gets because he has diabetes. If you knew Casey, it would be hard to picture him taking a back seat to anyone, much less diabetes. No matter what you do to try to keep things even, you can't help that your child with diabetes is going to get a kind of immediate attention that is medically necessary that your other children won't get. The hard part about having one child whose diabetes demands immediate attention at times is that it always seems to come at a time when your other child is looking for attention for something else. Usually you can't put off the demands of diabetes. That means that your "other child" is always getting put on the back burner. This is hard for that child to understand. From his point of view, it is his sibling who is coming before him, not the demands of diabetes.

We have already established that the demands of diabetes won't usually wait. So what can you do about that "other child"? You can put your non-diabetic child first whenever possible. Any time that the demands of diabetes do not need immediate attention, give your other child attention first. Especially at mealtime, give your non-diabetic child attention first whenever possible whether that means cutting his food first or asking about his day. Because mealtime is a particularly difficult time to do that, make the effort to do so whenever possible. Make a special effort to do things that focus on him whether it is cooking his favorite dinner or giving him your undivided attention.

If you have two children and are a two-parent household, divide and conquer. Have one adult talking or working with one child while the other two pair up. But don't keep those parent/child pairs the same. Switch the parent-child pairs, so each child gets individual attention from both parents, and parents get alone time with each child. You can also try to find something special to do with your non-diabetic child on a regular basis that will make the distribution of attention more equal.

Involve your non-diabetic child with the care of your diabetic child as much as possible. Tell him that he has an important job in the family. I tell Casey that he is my special helper when he and Joel go off to play alone together. I ask him to keep an eye on Joel to make sure he is looking or acting okay. This gets tricky if your diabetic child is the older one, as is the case in our situation. If you have trouble with this, try to carefully explain to your diabetic child how hard it is on your other child to always be left out when everyone else in the family is always talking about diabetes. It may make it easier on your diabetic child if he feels his sibling is being asked in order to make him feel included. Include your diabetic child's sibling in as many diabetes related events as possible. This will help make that child feel like diabetes isn't the source of all evil. In other words, having a brother with diabetes isn't so bad if it sometimes means you get to go to special camps, picnics and parties, and maybe even get free prizes. A lot of these events go out of their way to make siblings feel included. Seek out those types of events out and attend them. This year we are even going so far as to order "Casey's Cruisers" shirts for the breast cancer walk, to balance out the "Joel's Journey" shirts we have for the diabetes walk.

11

Equal Partners

Parents need to share the responsibilities of diabetes as equally as possible. This is not as easy as it sounds. I have heard a lot of parents talk about how their spouse won't do shots, doesn't know how to check for ketones, doesn't know anything about their child's insulin pump, etc. This is just plain wrong. Both parents need to be fluent in diabetes care, no exceptions. "We didn't choose this for our child, but we are in it together" should be every family's motto. Whether your have the same idea of how your child should eat, are married, divorced, or hate each other, your child's needs come first and you need to agree on that first.

When your child is first diagnosed with diabetes, the last thing on your mind is the division of labor between you and your spouse. However, it becomes an issue once you begin to develop a routine of daily diabetes care. Sometimes it becomes an issue because one spouse is doing all the work. Other times one parent is uncomfortable with certain aspects of their child's care. No matter what the reason, open and clear communication between you is the only way to work it out.

My husband and I have divided up the diabetes related jobs without even really talking about it. We each seemed to take on the jobs we were most comfortable with. My husband orders Joel's medical supplies, usually picks up his prescriptions, fills his pump cartridges and does most of his night-time testing. I do most site changes (Joel's choice, not mine), almost all preparation for and communication with school and most of the communication with his nurse at the Joslin Center. We share the responsibilities of carb counting, supervising bolusing and taking Joel to medical appointments.

This is not to say that we have not had our differences of opinion over who I think does how much of the work and whether or not it is fair and equal. First of all, none of it is fair. In a fair world, none of our children would have diabetes in the first place. But since we do have a child with diabetes, we have to figure out a way to get all the things done that need doing without anyone feeling like they are trying to manage all of it alone. This too is not easy. It helps if there are certain jobs that each of you feels most comfortable doing and you decide who does what on that basis.

My husband and I feel that it is important to allow and encourage Joel to do as much of his own care as possible. He has done that since the day he was diagnosed. The day after he was diagnosed he gave himself his first shot. He does all of his own blood testing and all of his own bolusing on his pump. His nurse Kathy set an outstanding precedent for this with how she taught us and him about diabetes care. She encouraged him to do things for himself from the first day, reminding us that it is his disease and that one day, he will be responsible for his own care. As hard as that is to imagine when your child is only 7, it is something that every parent needs to face. That is made a lot easier if your child is like Joel. He is very smart, independent, confident, brave and eager to learn new things. It helps all of us to feel that the whole family is in it together. Each of us feels less alone, and no one feels like he or she is doing all the work.

Just as it is important that everyone in the family is doing his or her part to care for your child, it is just as important that everyone recognizes when they, or someone other than yourself in the family needs a break. Sometimes it is easier to see when it is someone else who has had enough and needs to get away from it for awhile. But you also need to be able to speak up when it is you who needs the break. It is amazing what just an hour or two away from diabetes can do for you. Don't hesitate to lean on your spouse or the other members of your family and friends when you need to get a break. Chances are, if they haven't offered to give you a break, it is only because they haven't noticed that you need one. As I said in an earlier chapter, if you have trouble asking for help, you will need to get over it.

PART V

Walking the Tightrope

12

Gaining Control Without Obsessing

There is a very fine line between gaining control over your child's diabetes and obsessing over it. I am not claiming to know exactly where that line is, but as my husband recently said, "We have a much more normal life than I thought we would with Joel having diabetes." I agree with him. I am surprised by how normal our life feels. I feel like if we feel that way, and Joel's doctor is pleased with his A1C and blood sugars, we must be doing something right.

When Joel was first diagnosed he was underweight. He was thin to begin with and he had lost 5 pounds prior to his diagnosis. Once he got on insulin and began to feel better, his appetite was insatiable. I remember coming home from the grocery store and telling my husband I wasn't sure that we could afford Joel having diabetes. In those first few weeks, I spent hundreds of dollars on groceries. He gained 16 pounds in 6 weeks. He needed to gain the weight, but it was a drastic change. Because he was on shots at first, he had to snack at scheduled times so that we could basically "feed the insulin" that was in his body through his long-acting insulin. Over those first few months, his weight gain continued and became worrisome not only to us, but also to his nurse. We had to make some adjustments to his snacks, insulin and activity level. I became aware numerous times in those first few months how consuming this could become if we let it. This was not the first time that I made a conscious decision then that we weren't going to let it. Like so many things I have already covered in this book, that was easier said than done.

It is a balancing act of being careful, but not consumed; health conscious, but not obsessed; aware of what we are eating, without being totally preoccupied by it; knowing it is time to test, but not being completely rigid about it. This is not a balancing act you will likely master much sooner than around the first anniversary of your child being diagnosed with diabetes. If you are shooting for mastery sooner than that, you need to consider lowering your expectations. It is the kind of balance that comes from experience.

As I sit here trying to think of what tips I can offer about how not to obsess about diabetes, I've come up with some of the same things I have already mentioned in this book:

- **Take a break** from it, get out and take time for something you want to do that is fun.
- **Get support** from friends, family and especially other parents who have children with diabetes.
- **Read and learn about diabetes**. Be educated about what is okay to eat sometimes and what you really should avoid. Help your child come up with substitutions that are acceptable to both of you.
- **Remind yourself that the ups and downs of blood sugars are the nature of diabetes**. Having blood sugars that vary does not mean that your child's diabetes is out of control.
- **Let your child be a kid**. One of the best pieces of advice Joel's nurse Kathy has given me is to allow him to be like everyone else first, and correct his blood sugar later. The world will not come to an end if he eats a cupcake on an empty stomach.
- **Don't be a nag.** This is perhaps the toughest thing on this list to do. It is so hard not to nag your child about how much sugar and how many carbs he is eating. But I have come to realize that the more I do that, the more Joel hates having diabetes.
- **Let your child take charge of his diabetes**, as much as his age and maturity allows.

13

Be Proud of Your Child and Yourself

This is the chapter I have been most looking forward to writing. I feel good about what I do as a parent of a child with diabetes, and I would like to share that feeling with you. I'll bet if we each take a minute to think about the first days that our child had diabetes, there are at least ten things we wish we could do differently. Besides them never getting diabetes in the first place, there are so many things we wish we could undo. We have to let that go and know that we did the best we could at the time. Now we are doing even better. Don't judge yourself by how much you have yet to learn, be proud of how much you have already learned. And what about your child? Maybe he was hysterical that first day. But I'll bet he has made huge strides adjusting to having diabetes since then. Give yourself and your child credit for all that you both do every day just to survive life with diabetes. It is no small thing. I am guessing you don't often have someone tell you that, at least not as often as you need it. I am telling you now. You are an amazing parent for all that you have learned to do for your child. Your child is exceptional for dealing with this terrible disease. Whether they take it like a champ with no complaining, or scream like a baby, they are exceptional. So are you. We all are.

If you have trouble giving yourself a pat on the back, get over it. If you actually have a friend or family member who is sensitive enough to notice how well you manage your child's diabetes, AND she is thoughtful enough to say so out loud, don't dismiss it. Don't say something like, "Oh, it isn't that bad." First of all, we both know that is a lie. It sucks to have diabetes, and it sucks to have a child who has diabetes. Second, it just isn't fair to you. You deserve a little attention and praise for all that you do. Most people have no idea how many things you do every day just to manage you child's diabetes. If you have a friend who notices how well you are doing with all that you are juggling, look her in the eye and thank her for noticing how hard you are trying to hold it together. Thank her for being a great friend. If you don't have someone who is noticing and giving you that pat on the back that we all need, let your spouse know that you need him to recognize it and you will do the same for him when he needs it. If you don't have a spouse, turn to someone else who is close to you who you can talk to honestly about needing that little bit of praise.

When it comes to praising my child for handling having diabetes, I know that I err on the side of going overboard. I think this is a good thing. I never had to deal with something like this at my son's age, and I really can't imagine how hard it is, at his age, to be so different from everyone else. I marvel at how well Joel handles it, and I am never shy about telling him so. I also make a point to tell him in front of other people. It shouldn't be a secret how hard it is to have diabetes and it definitely shouldn't be a secret how well he is handling it. There are hundreds of ways you can let your child know how proud of him you are. If you do it right, maybe you will make him feel less bad about having diabetes. Shouldn't that be one of our main goals as parents? Here are a few of my favorite ways to show Joel I am proud of him:

- Write him a note saying I am proud of him.
- Tell him I am proud of him.
- Buy him a little something special.
- Buy him some diabetes "accessories" that make it more cool, like a cover for his pump, a new case for his supplies or an extra special medical ID bracelet.
- Encourage him to show other people how he tests or how his pump works.
- Buy him books for kids about having diabetes.
- Make an effort to meet other kids with diabetes.
- Ask him to help me teach other people about his diabetes.
- Go to a Family Diabetes Education Weekend.
- Go to diabetes camp.
- Go to a diabetes support group for kids and parents.

- Give him permission to say that diabetes sucks (when that is the only time we allow him to use a bad word. This is a tip that was shared with me by another parent.)
- Treat him like a regular kid, because he is one.
- Don't make everything about diabetes.
- Encourage him to do whatever he wants in life, regardless of diabetes.

14

Getting Away and Leaving Your Diabetic Child at Home

When you have a child who has diabetes, you feel like you are the only person who knows how to care for him, and in many ways that is probably true. You know what foods affect his blood sugar and how. You know how to calculate his carbs and boluses. You know the routine of how to give him shots or do site changes and how his correction scale works. You know how to test him in the middle of the night so he won't even wake up. These things all make it seem like you are the only person who can take care of him. But the truth is you are not as indispensable as you think you are. Every one of these things can be taught to another person. Even if you would rather do them yourself, or your child would prefer that you do them, they can be done by someone else.

Making the decision to leave home for overnight or longer is very difficult when your child has diabetes. But it goes back again to what message you want to give your child. Do you want him to think that he is so fragile that you always have to be there to keep him safe? Do you want him to think that he cannot take on at least some of the responsibility for his own care? Do you want him to think you and your spouse don't get to have a life outside of being parents? Hopefully you answered no to these questions. Even if you are terrified to leave your child with someone else, you need to ask yourself these questions and consider the message you are sending your child if you never leave him with someone else. No one is saying you need to do it in the first year, but you need to at least consider doing it at some point.

The year after my son was diagnosed I had the opportunity to earn a free trip through my home-based business. It meant leaving Joel and Casey with my Mom for 5 days and 4 nights. It was incredibly scary, not just for my husband and me, but for my mother! Before considering it too seriously, I asked Kathy (our nurse at Joslin) her opinion. She gave it to me straight, as she always does when she said, "There is absolutely no reason you can't go. In fact, it would be good for you if you did. There are a lot of parents who won't leave their diabetic child with anyone, and it isn't good for any of them." I love Kathy for so many reasons, but none more than for saying that to me.

At that point, I had 8 months to earn the trip and prepare to leave my son with my Mom. First I had to get her to agree to take on that responsibility, which I understood was very scary to her. She has told me many times that because she does not do things for Joel daily, she has trouble remembering what to do when. I decided that my first step was to create a book of information that she (and other babysitters) could refer to whenever they weren't sure what to do. It included many of the same things that my school folders contain: diabetes basics, what to bolus when, when bolusing is different (like right before exercise or bed-time), emergency phone numbers and instructions, etc.

Another thing it included was people she could call if there was a problem with Joel's infusion site (where his pump goes into his body). My Mom isn't able to put a site in, so I had to come up with someone who could do that for me while we were away. The natural choice was my sister-in-law Sandie, who is a nurse. She came over ahead of time to watch once, and then again to do one herself before we left. I also had two other people "on call" in case he needed an unscheduled site change in the middle of the night or at another time when Sandie couldn't make it (she lives 40 minutes away). I have a friend, Sandra, who is a nurse right down the street, and another diabetes parent was my other back-up person. My friend Maggie also offered to take the boys for a couple of play-dates to give my Mom a break while we were away.

I made sure that I had my "Joel folder" done a few months before our trip so that we could try it out to see what I had forgotten. I had both my Mom and Maggie try it out each time they babysat Joel to see what was missing. It was a good way to catch mistakes and items that had been omitted.

After that, I had to make sure that all my helpers were lined up and ready to go. My Mom had been spending a lot of time with us and had quite a bit of practice with supervising boluses and carb counting. She was nervous but ready. And so were we. It was the night before our big day to leave and Joel was nervous. He couldn't get to sleep that night and was anxious about us being away. I am not sure how much of it was directly related to diabetes and how much was basic separation anxiety, but at that point it didn't really matter. It was hard to leave knowing he was upset.

Going away meant more than just getting away from diabetes. It meant that there was a light at the end of the tunnel for us, that maybe our lives could be normal too. I know that one of the things I said in those first weeks after Joel was diagnosed was that we would never be able to leave home again. I really couldn't envision my Mom or anyone else being able to take over all the responsibility of monitoring Joel's diabetes if we were gone. But once the shock of his initial diagnosis faded and we got into a routine, we realized that we were not willing to accept never going away alone together. We also decided that was an unreasonable thing for any of us to concede.

So off we went, all the way from Syracuse, New York to Scottsdale, Arizona. Everyone did just fine. My Mom did an awesome job of taking care of Joel, and so did Joel. Sandie came and did his site change. We had a great trip, just the two of us. I can't possibly over-emphasize the importance of doing this. Taking a break really is one of the healthiest things you can do for all of you. It will also give all of you an enormous peace of mind and confidence about how well someone else can handle your child's care. (Thank you Mom for going outside of your comfort zone and giving us this wonderful gift by taking care of Joel and Casey for us while we were away!) Don't convince yourself that you are the only one who can take care of your child just because your child has diabetes. Once you do it the first time, you know that you can do it again!

While on this subject, we should talk about the more serious subject of the guardianship of your children. If you haven't already appointed guardians for your children, you really need to do so. Because you have a diabetic child this decision may be even more difficult. You would not only be leaving someone with the responsibility of raising your children, you would be leaving them with the added responsibility of raising a diabetic child. Here are some things to consider before even asking someone to be your child's guardian:

- Are they squeamish or uncomfortable around blood or needles?
- If so, are the willing and capable of getting past this?
- Does their lifestyle allow for frequent school nurse phone calls, going on school field trips, taking extra time to create school information forms, extra medical care and appointments, etc.?

- Do they have good health insurance?
- Do they currently show an interest in your child's diabetes?
- How many of their own children do they have?
- Will they approach your child's care the way you do so it is less change for your own child?
- Are your children comfortable with them?

PART VI
Common Ground

15

Diabetes Camps

The idea of a camp just for kids who have diabetes sounded strange to me at first. I think I had visions of them sitting around learning about diabetes all day, and I couldn't imagine what kid would want to spend their summer that way. If your child has ever been to a diabetes camp, you know that if there is one thing they do very little of at diabetes camps, it is sit around! Sometimes there is some diabetes education involved, but they sneak it in so the kids don't realize that they are learning. There is so much that kids get out of being surrounded by other kids who have diabetes. My son said it best after his first experience at diabetes camp: "When it is time to eat, everyone has to test. It is no big deal." It was like someone gave him back some of his normal life, because with everyone testing and having diabetes, he was "normal" in this setting.

Surrounding your diabetic child with other children with diabetes, even if it is only for a week, does something for them that no other experience can. It makes them less different from all the other kids. It shows them how other kids deal with having diabetes. It shows them that they are not alone.

The American Diabetes Association published a book, *Getting the Most Out of Diabetes Camp*, which I recommend. It covers things like why you should choose a diabetes camp, deciding if your child is ready, selecting the best camp, what to expect at camp, and more. It also has an appendix of diabetes camps by state to help you locate a camp in your area. I would strongly recommend this experience for your child with diabetes.

16

Getting Involved in Finding a Cure

I have never been much of a fundraiser and I have never liked asking people for money. But all that changed when I heard about the JDRF Walk to Cure Diabetes. I never felt like I could do enough to make a difference, compared to what I would like to do, to help fund research for a cure. The first year we walked, about 11 months after Joel's diagnosis, I decided to send an e-mail for donations and see what happened. We raised about $800 and had about 21 family members and friends walk with us. It was a great day and I think everyone was satisfied by the feeling that we were doing something to help raise money to find a cure.

Feeling a little more comfortable with the whole idea this year, I decided to send a letter by mail that included our group photo from last year's walk. The response was amazing. Our family alone raised over $2300 and our team raised over $5200. This year we had 35 walkers. There is something very powerful about knowing you are doing something that is really making a difference in finding a cure for diabetes. It is okay if you need to start out small. Just walk the first year with your family; ask for donations as you become more comfortable. Before you know it, you will have 100 friends and family members standing around in your team t-shirts having raised thousands of dollars for the cure.

If there is one thing every family affected by diabetes needs, it is hope. Hope for a cure. Let's find it together.

Thank you for letting me share my experience with you. I hope it has helped you in some way. If this book has had just one message, it is that you are not alone. It has been so helpful writing it because as I have written, I have realized I am not alone either. Please share your experience with another family affected by diabetes however and wherever you can, and together we will make it.

Glossary

Carbohydrate One of the primary sources of energy found in food; includes sugar, starch and fiber. Most carbohydrates induce a rapid rise in blood sugar levels.

Glucagon A hormone normally secreted by the pancreas; its primary action is to stimulate the liver to secrete glucose into the bloodstream. Glucagon is also a prescription medication that diabetics need to keep on hand in the case of an extreme low blood sugar. The glucagon is injected into the diabetic person who has lost consciousness.

Infusion Set The small apparatus used to deliver insulin below the skin by those wearing insulin pumps.

Infusion Site The location where an infusion set is injected into the body.

Insulin A protein hormone secreted by the islets of langerhans in the pancreas which helps the body use sugar and other carbohydrates.

Joslin Center A diabetes center named for the Joslin Family at which specialized endocrinologists care for the special medical needs of diabetes patients. There are 23 Joslin Diabetes Centers throughout the country.

Ketones Acid molecules produced during the breakdown of fat. Ketones can accumulate to dangerous levels in the absence of insulin as the body is unable to break down sugar for fuel.

Novolog A brand of fast acting insulin.

Shaky The feeling that a diabetic person sometimes has when experiencing a low (or sometimes high) blood sugar. This is an indicator to the person that he or she needs to test their blood sugar.

Children's Books About Diabetes Recommended by Joel Hargrave-Nykaza

Block, Jed. 1999. *The Best Year of My Life*. Appleton, WI: Jed Block.

Christopher, Matt. 1963. *Shoot for the Hoop*. New York, NY: Little, Brown and Company.

Dennis, Anne. 1998. *Taming the Diabetes Dragon*. Valley Park, MO: JayJo Books.

Gosselin, Kim. 1998. *Rufus Comes Home*. Valley Park, MO: JayJo Books.

Gosselin, Kim. 2002. *Taking Diabetes to School*. Plainview, NY: JayJo Books.

Gosselin, Kim. 1999. *Trick or Treat for Diabetes*. Valley Park, MO: JayJo Books.

Mazur, Marcia L., Peter Banks, and Andrew Keegan, eds. 1995. *The Dinosaur-Tamer*. Alexandria, VA: American Diabetes Association.

Peacock, Carol A., Adair Gregory, and Kyle Carney Gregory, eds. 1998. *Sugar Was My Best Food*. Morton Grove, IL: Albert Whitman & Company.

Roberts, Willo D. 1988. *Sugar Isn't Everything*. New York, NY: Aladdin Paperbacks.

Resources for Parents Recommended by Karen Hargrave-Nykaza

This is in no way a comprehensive list, but rather a list of books I have read so far and would recommend.

Books

Chase, Peter, H. M.D., 2002. *Understanding Diabetes,* 10th Edition. University of Colorado: University of Colorado Health Sciences Center.

Daneman, Denis, MB, BCh, FRCPC, Marcia Frank, RN, MHSc, CDE, and Kusiel Perlman, MD, FRCPC. 1999. *When a Child Has Diabetes.* Buffalo, NY: Firefly Books.

Hanas, Ragnar, M.D., PhD. 2005. *Type 1 Diabetes.* New York, NY: Marlowe & Company.

Kaplan-Mayer, Gabrielle. 2003. *Insulin Pump Therapy Demystified.* New York, NY: Marlowe & Company.

Loring, Gloria. 1999. *Parenting a Child with Diabetes,* second edition. Chicago, Illinois: Lowell House.

MacCracken, Joan, M.D. 1996. *The Sun, The Rain and The Insulin: Growing Up With Diabetes.* Orono, Maine: Tiffin Press of Maine.

McAuliffe, Alicia. 1998. *Growing Up with Diabetes: What Children Want Their Parents to Know.* New York, NY: Wiley & Sons.

Ogden, Abe. 2002. *Getting the Most Out of Diabetes Camp.* Alexandria, VA: American Diabetes Association.

Peurrung, Victoria. 2001. *Living With Juvenile Diabetes: A Practical Guide for Parents and Caregivers*. New York, NY: Hatherleigh Press.

Rubin, Alan L., M.D. 2001. *Diabetes for Dummies*. New York, NY: Wiley Publishing.

Scheiner, Gary, MS, CDE. 2004. *Think Like a Pancreas*. New York, NY: Marlowe & Company.

Wysocki, Tim, PhD. 1997. *The Ten Keys to Helping Your Child Grow Up With Diabetes*. Alexandria, VA: American Diabetes Association.

Zosel, Renea. 2003. *Diabetes: An Emotional Journey*. Covington, WA: Zay Publishing.

Websites

American Diabetes Association
www.diabetes.org

Barbara Davis Center for Childhood Diabetes
www.barbaradaviscenter.org

Children With Diabetes
www.childrenwithdiabetes.com

Juvenile Diabetes Foundation
www.jdrf.org
This is a good place to begin looking for information on support groups in your area.

Setebaid Services Inc.
www.setebaidservices.org

Bibliography

Because my book is anecdotal in nature it did not require much research in the traditional sense. I borrowed several of the glossary definitions I used from Gary Scheiner's book listed below.

Scheiner, Gary. *Think Like a Pancreas.* Marlowe & Company, 2004.

About the Author

Karen Hargrave-Nykaza has run a support group for parents of diabetic children, has been involved in teaching at several diabetes camps for children, has helped raise several thousands of dollars for the JDRF (Juvenile Diabetes Research Foundation) and has implemented a new protocol for diabetes care in her son's school system.

978-0-595-38841-7
0-595-38841-8

Printed in the United States
135895LV00001B/6/A

9 780595 388417